MY GREEN MANIFESTO

MY **GREEN** MANIFESTO

DOWN THE CHARLES RIVER
IN PURSUIT OF A
NEW ENVIRONMENTALISM

David Gessner

MILKWEED EDITIONS

Parts of *My Green Manifesto* were published in a different form in *Ecotone*,
OnEarth, and *Orion* magazine.

Milkweed Editions, 1011 Washington Avenue South, Suite 300,
Minneapolis, Minnesota 55415.
(800) 520-6455
www.milkweed.org

Published 2011 by Milkweed Editions
Printed in Canada
Cover design by Stewart A. Williams Design
Interior design by Wendy Holdman
The text of this book is set in Dante.
11 12 13 14 15   5 4 3 2 1
First Edition

Please turn to the back of this book for a list of the sustaining funders of
Milkweed Editions.

Library of Congress Cataloging-in-Publication Data

Gessner, David, 1961–
    My green manifesto : down the Charles River in pursuit
of a new environmentalism / David Gessner. — 1st ed.
        p.   cm.
    ISBN 978-1-57131-324-9 (pbk.)
        1. Environmentalism.   2. Environmental protection.
    3. Environmental protection—Massachusetts—Charles
    River   4. Environmentalism—Massachusetts—Charles River.
    5. Charles River (Mass.)—Description and travel.   I. Title.
        GE195.G47 2011
        304.2—dc22

                                              2011012994

This book is printed on acid-free paper.

To Hadley Gessner, Again and Always

A man does best when he is most himself.

        —*Henry David Thoreau*

It's not that easy being green.

        —*Kermit the Frog*

MY GREEN MANIFESTO

PRELUDE: THE RIVER MAN   5

I.   THE SOURCE
     A Backyard Wilds   13
     A New Music   21
     The Fire This Time   27
     Fighting Words   39

II. A LIMITED WILD
     Environmental Extremists   55
     The Myth of Dan   67
     A Larger Fight   75
     The Wild West   85
     The Irish Alehouse   99

III. TRANSFORMATION
     The Vision Thing   115
     Bird Men   127
     Antaeus   139
     Island Boys   149
     Dan's River   157
     Flight   165

IV. INDEPENDENCE DAY
     Henry's River   177
     Hey, Hey We're the Monkeys   189
     Fireworks   199
     Beyond   213

POSTLUDE: THE END OF THE WORLD   219

ENDNOTES   223

MY GREEN MANIFESTO

"DIRTY WATER"

—Ed Cobb

I'm gonna tell you a big fat story, baby
Aww, it's all about my town

Yeah, down by the river
Down by the banks of the river Charles
Aw, that's what's happenin' baby
That's where you'll find me
Along with lovers, buggers and thieves
Aw, but they're cool people

Well I love that dirty water
Oh, Boston you're my home

'Cause I love that dirty water
Oh, Boston you're my home (oh, yeah)[1]

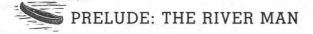 PRELUDE: THE RIVER MAN

We are paddling our rock-battered canoe down a particularly stunning section of the river, twisting between steep granite walls and overhanging trees, as we travel toward the hidden city at river's end. Over the past hours we have heard coyotes howl and watched deer wade, observed a sharp-shinned hawk swoop into the canopy, swallows cut above the water in front of us, kingfishers ratchet past, and toasted with beers to congratulate ourselves after an exhilarating ride through rapids. If I squint I can imagine myself on a great and wild river, the Amazon or Congo or, at least, the Colorado, and can imagine the man steering the canoe behind me as an epic adventurer, Teddy Roosevelt, say, hurtling down the River of Doubt.

The truth is slightly less glamorous. The truth is this isn't the Amazon but the Charles—a name that conjures up images less adventurous and wild than fancy and effete, not to mention domesticated and decidedly *British*—and that the hidden city ahead is known, in the native tongue, as *Bawhston*. What's more, the dwellings we will soon pass will not be primitive huts but Super Stop & Shops, and the *Homo sapiens* we'll encounter downriver will not be headhunters but Harvard students, and, if I am perfectly honest, the fearless leader in the stern isn't Teddy R. but a state worker named Dan Driscoll, who I once played some Ultimate Frisbee with, and who we referred to, in those days, as "Danimal."

We like to strip down myths, we modern folk, and it's easy enough to quickly strip our journey of all its mythic qualities: to see it as a pretty modest trip on a pretty modest river with a modest enough guy. But if our adventure has not been a life-or-death journey into a vast, untamed wilderness, the truth is I have been consistently astonished over the last couple of days, not just by the hidden wildness of the river but by Driscoll himself. The man's own considerable energy, which I had only previously witnessed when he chased down Frisbees like a border collie, is equally apparent when he talks about his efforts to revitalize the river we travel down.

"It started back around 1990 when I was working as a planner for the state," he tells me as we paddle. "Someone in the office said 'Why don't you take a look at the Charles?' I think they were just trying to give the new kid something to do. Little did they know. I looked over the maps and saw possibilities. I began to plan and scheme. When I first started talking about connecting the river paths, everyone looked at me like I was crazy. I said, 'Let's have these green paths that run through the urban areas. Let's re-plant native plants to bring animals back. Let's reconnect people to nature.' Pretty soon I was known as this raging ecological planner. . . . Next thing I knew I was 'The River Man.'"

Dan Driscoll is a man of average height and proportions, fit and compact, thanks in part to his daily bike commute in and out of Boston. Since our Frisbee days his hair has gone white, but his intense eyes still shine out a cracked blue. There is something of the true believer to Dan, as there has to be in anyone who will take on the sort of fight he has; but that intensity is leavened by a certain regular guy-ness and sense of humor.

As he paddles, he describes what he calls his "radical idea" that being environmental isn't about education or politics. It's about what Thoreau called "contact." Falling in love with something— a place, an animal—and then fighting for it.

"When I grew up in Newton we always had our butts dragged out to Lincoln to learn about 'nature.' The way I look at it, if one kid walks out into his *own* backyard and has contact with nature, then maybe that will do something. Maybe he'll be inspired to fight for the place. Maybe he'll be the next John Muir."

He pauses to correct his exaggeration.

"Or at least maybe he'll just be less of a dick."

Environmentalism is officially hot the summer we paddle down the river. Not long ago Arnold Schwarzenegger posed as a green warrior on the cover of *Newsweek*, while a couple of spots down the magazine rack *Vanity Fair* featured Leo DiCaprio standing next to a young polar bear on what I assume was meant to be a melting iceberg. In a few months Al Gore will win a shiny new Oscar for showing us his slide show. In the meantime, celebrities everywhere are tripping over themselves trying to show off their small carbon footprints.

Many of us understand that the things environmentalists have long told us are right. Though we don't actually do it, we know that we should eat and drive less. And, on a deeper level, we know that we should conserve. We the people need to move away from our obsession with growth at all costs toward a dependence on local economies, and obviously away from slurping down oil and gobbling resources like a bunch of drunken gluttons. Yes, we *know;* we *understand.* But all these *shoulds* and *needs.* What about *wants* and what about *fun?* We are Americans for God's sake!

Why does environmentalism, much of which is just common sense, so often sound like nagging? Particularly deadening is the endless repetition of the phrase "global warming." We have all seen Uncle Al's slideshow and are appropriately horrified. But what to do? Certainly the answer doesn't lie only in screwing in those twisty little light bulbs. Whatever the answer is, it isn't singing the same songs to the same choir. Maybe it's overstatement to say that environmentalism, for all the recent media coverage, has lost its soul, but it's not an overstatement to say that it has lost its power to excite the masses, or, at least, to excite me. And if it can't excite me, the card-carrying nature guy among my friends, then environmentalism is in trouble.

For my part, while I have spent a lot of time in the natural world and can talk almost unblushingly about my love for it, I've always been uncomfortable with the "environmentalist" label. Then again, all my hair splitting might just be a case of playing Hamlet when what the world needs is action. Whatever we call ourselves, it is time to *do something.* But what to do when there are so damned many catastrophes, and how to do it without playing out the same old environmentalist Chicken Little act?

I will not insult you, dear reader, and pretend, for the sake of narrative, that Dan Driscoll is a folksy sage who holds the answers to all these questions. But I will say that, even before I put my paddle in the water, I am starting to think that Dan may hold hints of what I am rooting around for. It occurs to me that Dan might just be the right eco-hero for these times. Not an oversized Arnold Schwarzenegger or a Vulcan-like Al Gore, or even a Teddy Roosevelt in the Amazon, but a regular guy fighting a local fight for a limited wilderness—the only sort of wilderness available to most of us. Maybe what is needed isn't a raging prophet of doom, a stern-faced administrator, or an action hero, but a slightly goofy, stubborn, joyful, ex-Frisbee playing stoner of modest proportions—a stubborn guy who fell in love with a place and then fought like hell for it.

$$\times$$

Life is strange: the way you sometimes start in one place and float elsewhere, seemingly despite—or even without—the self you once were. Dan Driscoll couldn't have possibly plotted out becoming "The River Man" on a graph, moving from point A to B. As for me, I never set out to become that animal known as a nature writer. Little did I know. But one thing led to another and over the last dozen years I have written six books where the natural world—and birds in particular—keeps sneaking in, while being christened with tenure and the dubious title of "environmental spokesperson." At the same time I have found myself unhinged over a seemingly simple question: How does any individual—swamped with other concerns and worries—wrestle their way toward a relationship with place and, perhaps, a means of fighting for that place? It isn't an easy question for me to answer, and I assume that this is also true for you, swamped as you likely are with your job, your family, your life. And so I thought that I, newly a father and overwhelmed with work, might be the right person to help answer the question. Which led me to set out to do what anyone would do in such a bind: write a manifesto.

What I didn't realize was that most issuers of manifestos begin with their conclusions concluded, their concrete
hardened, and their intentions, motives, and views firmly in
mind, or in hand, fit to bash you over the head with. I began,
on the other hand, with nothing more than questions—
questions as numerous as the sources of the Charles River,
and as meandering as the river itself. But trust, dear reader,
that though these questions do wander, they also reach
the sea, moving toward answers if not the answer.

In this small book I have welded that intellectual
adventure to the physical one of riding the wild Charles
with Dan. Perhaps the two were not always as concur-
rent as they appear in the text (I did not carry a lectern
in my canoe, after all) but the two journeys informed
each other so deeply that I present them here as one.

And last, while my thoughts may flow from many
sources, Dan Driscoll's spring directly from the man himself: On the trip I carried a tape recorder wrapped in a
zip-lock bag, which means that Dan Driscoll's words are his
own—with the "ums" and "ands" edited out. And of course
the amazing feats of derring-do we indulge in, heroically
taming the wild river, are also entirely true and factual.

I. THE SOURCE

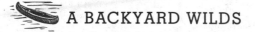 A BACKYARD WILDS

The original plan had been for Dan and me to paddle the entire river together, but it turned out that for Dan the business of fighting for the Charles takes precedence over the pleasure of floating on it. A state meeting interfered, so I am paddling the first day solo.

Earlier this morning, however, Dan took some time away from work to drop me off at the launch, driving way too fast down the back roads of Medfield and Norfolk while we drank tubs of Dunkin' Donuts coffee. He explained that the kayak I'd be paddling was an expensive one and not really his but a loaner from a friend. As it turned out he was nervous enough about me navigating my first rapids that he drove to the Pleasant Street Bridge to coach me through the initial series of rocks. He was right to be nervous as I had mostly kayaked on ocean marshes before and, while the rapids on the Charles pale before true river rapids, they were challenging enough to do damage to the boat, if not to me.

Dan stared down from the bridge above, no doubt wincing when I slammed full on into a half-submerged boulder. After that I self-consciously picked my way along until, at last, I landed in a strong trough of current that whooshed me away and down the river.

That was how it started. Six hours have passed since then and I have not seen another canoe or kayak. What I have seen is a dazzling array of birds—hawks, wrens,

warblers, orioles, tanagers, woodpeckers — and a variety of
landscapes that not even the most optimistic nature lover
would expect only miles from the tenth largest metropolitan area in the United States. After the exhilaration of the
early rapids, I found myself riding a current of tannin-dark
water that reflected back the overgrown banks of maple,
swamp oak, and beech. Several miles later, the river began
to double and triple back on itself, twisting and turning
through the great marsh that divides Millis and Medfield,
a landscape filled with the rustling of tall phragmite grass
and the whistle-*skreek* punchlines of red-winged blackbirds.

The day's weather has been as variable as the landscape
with great cloud continents shifting overhead. At one moment I am paddling in scorching midsummer sun, shirt
off and sweating, and the next I find myself in the midst
of a rain shower. All the while water bugs play across the
river, pock-marking the surface along with the raindrops.
As I float past, painted turtles plop off the mud banks,
swallows swerve above the river hunting for insects, fish
jump, and at one point I watch a beaver plow by with a
sprig of vegetation in its mouth, leaving a V wake behind.

I half-expected something like this, but not really
like *this*. What I'm trying to say is that while I knew
this trip would be kind of wild — if I hadn't I wouldn't
have signed on in the first place — what I didn't expect
was the sheer thrill of the experience, the thrill of being
alone and discovering a new place, a thrill that reminds
me of my first time stumbling upon an Anasazi ruin
while hiking through the desert in southeastern Utah.
Not that it is as spectacular and novel as that, at least
to my Eastern eyes, but the experience itself has held
the same bubbling thrill. Part of this comes from the

fact that I expected more houses and human intrusion.
Occasionally I'll notice a dock or rowboat that indicates
I'm paddling through someone's backyard, but more
often the feeling is one of relative solitude with little
indication that I am entering the home turf of over four
million human beings. Furthermore, the evidence of
human habitation, however minimal, is, in its own way,
as thrilling as the long sections of trees. What you see
of the houses has a secret childhood feel to it: that rope
swing out over the river, the old dock with a dinghy
tied up to it, those decayed stairs leading to the water.
None of the lawns are of the enormous and mowed
variety, and the few houses themselves are only glimpses
through the branches and leaves. I can't help but think
how lucky the people are who live there, lucky to have
a river moving like a dream through their backyards.

My point here is not to describe the lovely world, but rather
to make some points about saving it. And yet, oddly, my
first point is that the world *is* still lovely, even when it is
limited and somewhat un-wild. In other words, for all of
environmentalism's cries of doom, there are still places like
this river, teeming with life and flowing right through our
backyards. Yes, the world is overheating, and, yes, we will
get to that; but how about—before the flames of apocalypse
consume the planet—we explore our own neighborhoods
a little?

I think of my friend Bill Roorbach, whose house in
Farmington, Maine I visited not long ago. The house itself
was nothing special, at least not at first glance: a crowded
two-story dwelling with warped floors that sat right on

a paved road. But when he took me out into the backyard, I began to understand why you couldn't shut him
up about the place. Behind the house, there grew a great
shambling garden and that was just for starters. From
the garden we walked along a path through the briars
and woods, "down to the stream," he said, but when we
reached the water, which I was expecting to look very
docile — all quaint and New-Englandy — it was nothing like a stream. The small woods opened up and we
were standing in front of a powerful surge of wide water,
water that S-ed around and cut deeply into the opposite
bank, water that looked more like a Western river than
a New England brook. Instantly it became clear why he
had brought me there, why he had showed me this before
showing me his living room or study or anything else
inside. He pointed to it with pride and without a word
I got it. *This is where I live,* he was saying, *This is why I live
here. This is where I come to gather myself, be myself, and get
beyond myself. This is where I come to get to know my neighbors,
neighbors that include birds and beavers and muskrats and an
occasional moose or fisher. And this is where I come to connect
to the greater world since this un-stream-like stream eventually
flows into the river and then that river flows into the ocean.*

Well, his backyard is extraordinary, you might argue, as
was Henry David Thoreau's backyard, which held Walden
Pond. But I think that is exactly the wrong point to take
away. As a kid who grew up in Massachusetts, I can tell you
that ponds like Walden are a dime a dozen, a few hundred
others just like it scattered around the state. "Oh, it's nothing special!" people often say when they first see the pond.
Which is the whole beautiful point! It's as ordinary as it gets,

and that is why it's so important. It means that your own
ordinary backyard might just be extraordinary, too. It means
that *your* own territory might also be worth exploring.

✕

When most people think of the Charles, if they think of it
at all, they imagine a tame and preppy river, a river that got
into the Ivy League, a river of boathouses and scullers. But
when Captain John Smith spied the Charles from Boston
Harbor in 1614, he wasn't thinking about scullers or tea
parties or final clubs.[2] Like any explorer worth his salt, his
dreams were of discovery—the main chance—and in the
river he thought he'd hit upon it. He took one look at its
great gaping mouth and assumed that it was a raging torrent
of water that cut deep into the continent. It turned out he
was spectacularly wrong in this assumption: not only does
the river not reach halfway to California, it barely makes it
halfway to Worcester. What Smith had not anticipated was
that the Charles, like many people, has a mouth too big
for its body. His disappointment over the river's length did
not stop him from naming it after his king, forever saddling
the poor river with a name that is stiff and a little goofy.
Imagine the difference if he had called it "The Chuck."

As for the river's length, it covers, as the crow flies
from source to mouth, about twenty-six miles, almost
exactly the same distance as the Boston Marathon. This
makes sense since the Charles, like the Marathon, begins
in the town of Hopkinton. The difference is that the river,
unlike the runners, isn't interested in traveling straight
and fast. By the time it wends its way to the harbor it has
actually covered something closer to eighty miles, earning

its Indian name of Quinobequin which means "meander." That name is currently under debate, as is the river's actual source—the good folks of Milford claim the river starts in their town, not in Hopkinton—but most agree that it emerges in the latter town, as my own observations confirm.

✕

I had agreed to drive Dan's boats from Cape Cod to his house in Boston, but, a born meanderer myself, before delivering the boats I had to go to Hopkinton to search for the river's beginnings. With a large canoe and a kayak atop my car, I rattled down Granite Street, where I observed small muddy creeks trickling into a manmade reservoir named Echo Lake. I couldn't see how to get into the lake since the woods were posted with signs that said NO TRESPASSING: TOWN OF MILFORD WATER SUPPLY, and I couldn't very well leave Dan's kayak and canoe unwatched, so I drove up a smaller street until I saw a woman in her front yard washing her car. I've always relied on the kindness of strangers, and sure enough when I pulled into the driveway and got out to say hi, the woman immediately pointed at the kayak and told a story about a recent canoe trip she'd been on. Her name was Amy Markovich and she ran a business called Echo Lake Adirondacks which sold the elegant wooden chairs that were displayed on her lawn. She was delighted that I was going to paddle the length of the Charles, and rushed inside to print out aerial photos of the lake, displaying them for me as though she were showing off pictures of her children. After she put the pictures away, she coached me on the best way to hike into the reservoir. She seemed

genuinely proud to have this mysterious thing—the
very source of the Charles—in her own backyard.

She let me leave the car in her driveway and promised
to keep an eye on the boats. I followed her instructions
and hiked back down the road before cutting in on the
ATV trails as she'd suggested. After about a mile I came
upon the lake, which gave me my first hint that there was
a hidden wilderness within the confines of Boston's suburbs. It's true that my initial sight was of a pile of litter at
the base of a red cedar—Coors empties, water bottles,
and a Newman's Own salad dressing bottle, as if these
had been particularly health-conscious litterbugs—but
what I saw next was the blue bowl of the lake itself. Silver
shined through the birch and pine and, with its many
small coves, you could easily imagine you were looking
out at a lake in Maine or Canada. I tramped around for a
while—following deer tracks in the mud, listening to a
kingfisher overhead—and tried to determine the indeter-
minable: Which of those muddy brooks, barely trickles
now in early summer, was the true source of the Charles?

After hiking out, I thanked Amy, promised to dedicate
a chapter to her, then drove back down Granite Street
and pulled over by a mossy graveyard to study the brooks
to the north of the reservoir. These nameless incarna-
tions are the first drops of what eventually will become
the Charles—a truly modest beginning to a great river.[3]

On the other end of the reservoir, the water dribbled
out of Echo Lake and along Route 85, next to Wendy's
and Pizza 85, gradually picking up force and momentum.
But only *gradually*. If you judged this river just from its
beginnings you would have to conclude that it would

never amount to much; a shiftless townie river that wasn't going anywhere much less the Ivy League. Unambitious, it seemed destined to do no more than dribble behind the strip malls of Milford. Of course I knew that the river, like a lot of us, would overcome its muddled beginnings.

 A NEW MUSIC

For the better part of the morning and into the afternoon a great blue heron waits then flies off in front of
me, waits and flies off again, engaging me in a marathon
game of tag. I first saw the bird not long after the initial
rapids on the left bank by some turtles, and its size startled
me. To real bird watchers, great blue herons, which have
done surprisingly well in the face of continued habitat
destruction, have lost some of their appeal due to the
fact that they are fairly common. But, all alone and drifting up close to the bird with its full six-foot wingspan, I
was reminded that it had earned the "great" in its name.

Our game goes like this: I try to paddle by as quietly
as possible, but inevitably the bird periscopes its long neck
up, tightens as I approach, then rocks back slightly before
leaping into the air. The pre-leap moment is a tense one for
the bird and part of my game is trying to guess the exact
second it will launch itself into the sky. Often this depar-
ture is accompanied by a loud, pissed-off sounding *sproak*.
Of course I know I am anthropomorphizing: If the bird
really is pissed off, why does it keep flying downstream
from me instead of simply heading upstream a little and
letting me go by? I don't know the answer to this, but if
I'm an irritant to the bird, then it is anything but to me.
Each time it flies off I study its deep, slow flapping, its long
neck pulled back into its chest. It looks graceful, ghostly,
and ungainly all at once. A gray vision except for its chest,

which seems to absorb whatever blue the reflected river offers. Even more than its size, its wing beat — so muscular and deliberate it looks like it is paddling through a substance more viscous than air — distinguishes it. The heron glides ahead to the next stop and the game continues.

$$\times$$

Pardon me for going on so long about a bird. These things happen when you are alone on a river. As it turns out though, Dan Driscoll has a thing for great blue herons, too. Dan can sound hardheaded and funny when discussing the Red Sox or the idiocy of state bureaucracy, but, like a lot of us, including me, his language sometimes goes soft when it turns to nature.

Last night I slept over at Dan's house in Watertown, and during the late innings of the Sox game, after a few too many beers, he began to talk about nature as his "only religion," and admitted that the great blue heron was something close to his "totem bird." I squirmed a little at that, and he backed off.

"Well, at the very least, it served as a kind of mascot," he said.

$$\times$$

The heron's body is the blue of stains from old-fashioned carbon paper. The blue darkens to something close to black at the wingtips, lightened only by a white splash of feathers — the heron's "headlights" as birders call them — between the two tones. I see it near a small side creek, periscope up, on alert, then retracted enough to completely change the metaphor: now neck and head look like a curled-back hand puppet. The primary feathers are more blue than the rest, the secondaries more gray, and together they create a color uniquely heron. Shining yellow eyes are circled by rings of black, but between eye and mask there is smaller circle of color: a whitish yellow that seemed to run like a bad watercolor down into the bill. At first the bird appears completely motionless, but then I notice the bill slowly opening and closing, as if it is whispering to itself. The wind ruffles the heron's feathers slightly, but other than the bill, and the slightest shifts in posture, it stays still. Then, suddenly, it twists its head around and its bill flashes like the blade of a knife.

When I take a break and look down at my field guide, it tells me that herons are colonial nesters, gathering together at night after days spent on their own. This strikes me as odd, counterintuitive. Herons always seem prickly about their privacy; they like their space, as the saying goes. My trouble reconciling the bird's love of solitude with the fact of colonial nesting clears up when I read further down the page: Heron social life, like human social life, varies from season to season. For humans, summer is often the most social time, and the same holds true for herons. In summer they live in colonies and disperse to fish their own waters during the day; in winter they are on their own all the time, becoming territorial about their space. Part-time outgoing and part-time antisocial. A rhythm I could live with.

✕

I mentioned that Dan's words grew soft and mushy when he began to talk about nature. Perhaps I am too persnickety, too preoccupied with the language that he, or any of us, uses to describe the natural world, but I am in the minority that believes we should watch our words, that false language both reflects and encourages false thinking, that our lives depend on our sentences. I feel particularly strongly that "being in nature" should not be described as some precious or highfalutin experience. After all, didn't we as a species evolve, along with our words, while spending a million years or so living in the midst of the natural world? And wasn't our relationship with that world, among other things, quite practical and direct? "Nature" is where the living roots of our language evolved, which suggests that that language should still be able to circle back and describe the place from whence we came. Like the natural world itself, natural language has become fenced-off and attenuated. Our words are zoo animals.

So many people who speak for the wild world seem to feel the need to speak in the voice of the mystic, a hushed, voice-over reverence. We affect this high priest tone, and everyone else is expected to get down on their knees and listen to the whispered wisdom of the shaman. At times like those there's very little indication that any of us have the quality that many humans find most important for living on earth: a sense of humor. You'd never guess that any of us ever laughed or farted. (Which, it needs to be pointed out, is different than translating Native American myths about trickster coyotes who laugh and fart.)

I cringe when my language grows too flaccid on the one hand—*oh, Great Blue Heron, help my soul and keep all sweetness and light*—or, on the other, too rigid and devoid of feeling—*Great Blue Heron, or* Ardea herodias, *a member of the order* Ciconiiformes.

Lately, I've been invited to give a lot of talks, and when I speak people sit listening, rapt, or at least putting on rapt faces. I suppose if I really wanted to make it big I

would start spreading the word of doom and intoning
the phrase "global warming" over and over, hitting my
audiences with it like a big stick. But I've got other ideas,
however, *impure* and pesky little ideas that get in the way.
For instance, sometimes I think that, from an artistic point
of view, the end of the world might be kind of *interesting*, at least more interesting than all the dull predictions
about it. Another troubling notion is that I'm not really
sure I want to be this thing called an environmentalist.

I'm not trying to be glib here — I don't think it's unim-
portant to fight for environmental causes. It's just that I
would like to put forth a sloppier form of environmentalism, a simultaneously more human and wild form, a more
commonsense form and, hopefully, in the end, a more effective form. Because the old, guilt-ridden, mystical enviro-
speak just isn't cutting it. Maybe the musty way of talking
about nature needs to be thrown over a clothesline and
beaten with a broom. That's what I've been trying to say at
these talks I've been giving. My role, as I see it, is to try to
pull the pole out of the collective environmental ass. It isn't
easy work. For a costume I wear a Hawaiian shirt and to get
into character I drink a few beers. Throughout my talks I
make jokes about how earnest everyone is and the audience
usually laughs along semi-masochistically. Sometimes I get
carried away. I start feeling megalomaniacal and believe I
am the bringer of a new language. I imagine myself to be
Bob Dylan at Newport, playing electric guitar among the
folkies, trying (futilely) to get them to yell out "Judas."

This last metaphor was confirmed by one of the
door prizes I was given recently, a CD tribute to Rachel
Carson's work, after a talk at a conference in Boothbay
Harbor, Maine to celebrate Carson's life and work. On

the way home I listened to a song on the CD that told the
story of the osprey's near demise from DDT and then
its remarkable comeback, a subject I once wrote a book
about. It is fair to say that Carson is one of my greatest
heroes but the music that came warbling out of my speak-
ers seemed to be sung by a caricature of a late fifties Pete
Seeger wannabe, who wailed about the poisons coursing
through the ospreys' bodies with such excruciating earnestness that it almost made me root for the birds' death.
Anything as long as the song ended. This, I found myself
thinking, *this* is part of the problem. Why does nature
turn us into this kind of warbler? It makes me long for a
new sort of music, a music with energy, irreverence, and
drive, a punk osprey tribute sung by, say, the Sex Pistols.

And maybe, I think now, that's a good place to start.

A new music.

 THE FIRE THIS TIME

I paddle through the afternoon, watching the pulsating light
on the under branches of trees. Somewhere on the other
side of this living green wall cars are rushing to and from
the city, but that doesn't concern me. How many types
of weather can I name from the day? Too many to count.
The wind comes up, the water ripples, the clouds blow
over and create a chill, then disappear; after the sun bears
down, the wind stops, and a short rain falls. Every turn of
the river is different. There is no formula for it. As I slide
past the forested banks whole riverside landscapes reflect in
the water. The cloud continents rush overhead and the rain
soaks me again. Shaggy weeping willows bow to the river.

What would a new environmental music sound like?
It might, at the risk of coming off like the mystics I just
ridiculed, sound a bit like this river. Burbling, lapping,
rushing, calm, excited, but above all *fluid*. And contradic-
tory, too, rushing one way but filled with back eddies and
counter-currents. Uncertain and confident all at once.

Before I go all Siddhartha on you, however, let me
add that it should also be blunt. Wedging downward past
nineteenth-century romanticism and tunneling back toward
the practical source of "nature language": daily dialogues
with fellow tribesmen, directions to the kill, songs sung by
generations upon generations of roaming hunter-gatherers.
Ugh. Wolf scat. Look—berries. That's a kind of music, too.

Of course it's hard to keep a fluid, riverlike mind in this

time of adamancy and increased hysteria. We live in an age
of blowhards, windbags, and he-who-shouts-loudest wins.
In the environmental community this means increasingly
shrill warnings about our pending doom. We are never allowed, not for a moment, to forget GLOBAL WARMING
and its corollary admonishment that we must SAVE THE
WORLD. While I know it is sacrilege to say it, I still don't
believe that "global warming" is the answer to every question left on earth. Frankly, the subject exhausts me. I find
my optimism and energy waning when my brain turns to
that ever-popular environmental topic: *The End of the World.*
Perhaps that is because I, like most of us, am not built to
think in terms of the apocalypse. Too much of it and I am
left stunned, helpless, curled up in a fetal position on the
kitchen floor.

It's not that I disagree with the experts. If they are right,
and they probably are, the next century will be a dismal one.
Our present six billion will become ten. Our resources will
dry up as the world warms and our population essentially
doubles. Massive extinctions are likely to occur—in fact,
they are already occurring—animals that have inhabited the
planet for millions of years will be gone forever. The truth is
that it's great to care about sentences and write books and all,
but I'm not sure anything is going to help. If the predictions
are even half-correct, we're fucked.

I admire all the thinkers who try to wrestle with these
concepts and come up with ideas that will help. I admire
all those brave enough to try and offer words and solutions. But for my part, I can't help but despair. I'm out of
my league really, and in that I'm not so unlike most of us.
When it comes to politics, I have no global plan or solution. I'm sorry. It is not what I'm good at and maybe it's

not what the animals that we evolved into are good at. One of the religious purposes for the concept of an apocalypse was to force us to admit that life was terrifying beyond the ken of mere human beings. And it *is* beyond the ken.

If you are like me, there is something particularly unpleasant about the fashion of apocalypse currently in vogue. At least with nuclear annihilation everything would end quickly. And at least it wouldn't so obviously be each of our own *faults*. Our current fantasy of disaster has a distinctly unpleasant aspect in that we should all feel *personally* responsible. *For the end of the world.* Drive your car too long or take a hot shower and you're contributing to the great, final doom.

It isn't just about feeling guilty either. I question the effectiveness of using the nagging tone in which so many of these announcements of doom are broadcast. You may find yourself wishing that, even if the doomsday predictions are entirely accurate (down to the last minute and extinction), even if our fate is sealed (or, *almost* sealed as they always like to say, giving us a last second chance at reform), even if it is all true (and I, for one, will admit it is true, more or less), even if all this is the case could we just SHUT THE FUCK UP ABOUT IT FOR A MINUTE? Could we at least take a week off from new projections of doom? A month off from talk of the apocalypse? Maybe even a year-long moratorium on books that begin with the words *The End of, The Death of,* or *The Last*?

I will be accused of wanting to bury my head in the sand. But I don't want to bury my head; I just want a short fucking break to remember that there are good parts about being alive. I am not Henry David Thoreau, I get that, and I live in a limited, depraved, depressing time; but I am here to say that I can still experience joy and yes, maybe even a little transcendence, even when watching a river that is flowing behind a Stop & Shop. I don't want to act naïvely, but I do want an environmentalism that I can live with; one that is a part of my everyday life, not running roughshod over it. Imagine living with a spouse who feels the need to scream, several times a day, "THIS MARRIAGE IS OVER! WE'RE DOOMED!" It's not so different than being part of a group that is always erupting with, "THE WORLD IS ENDING!" Yes, okay, sure, we know it's doomed, but could we just be quiet for a while, watch some TV maybe, go for a walk? Nothing is going to get better overnight, so maybe it's time to think about a more effective way of shouting?

What I am arguing against, I suppose, is an environmentalism that feels like the intellectual equivalent of a panic attack. Doesn't it make sense to work toward a more integrated environmentalism, incorporating our selves, our worlds; a saner, calmer, more commonsensical environmentalism; an environmentalism that accounts for quirks, hypocrisy, nuance, comedy, tragedy? Of course even as I write these words I hear the counter argument, the argument of that imagined shrill spouse: "WHAT THE HELL ARE YOU TALKING ABOUT? HOW CAN YOU HAVE SOME SORT OF *LAID-BACK APPROACH* TO THE END OF THE WORLD?"

$$\times$$

It's not too hard to see why most of us don't spend a lot of time dwelling on these larger issues. Who wants to feel that knot in their chest, that twisting in their gut? The feeling of panic I get about the state of the world is not so different, on a personal, physical level, from the tightness I experience when worked up about the state of my own finances.

Paddling, it turns out, is a fairly effective way to shut up one's mind. Dan did a lot of it in those first days working for the state, getting to know the river he would soon be fighting for. Today, paddling helps me turn from brain to body. Whatever else kayaking is, it is a form of work, and work, starting with the taking of small actions, is the only reliable way I know to escape from those insomniac anxieties that can strike even in broad daylight. In this case, that means rotating my paddle in and out of the water. Feeling the sun on my face, the sweat trickling down my neck as I paddle harder. Not that this is truly a "way out" of the problem, not that my paddling will help with global warming in any way or form. But it is a break, a respite, before returning fresh.

And before long I *am* feeling good. My thoughts calmer, my muscles stronger. Birds also help pull me outward. I watch the flashing blue backs of swallows as they skim over the water, scooping up insects in mid-flight as I paddle through a channel some forty feet wide, between banks high with grasses, viburnum, and the occasional willow tree. Through my binoculars I can study the flight of one particular swallow, intrigued by its mussel-orange belly, trying to trace its every turn and twist, and then, concentrating even more deeply, trying to anticipate where it will turn or bank next. I can actually watch the moment it opens its bill and snaps — the exact moment it catches a damselfly out of the air. I follow the bird with my gaze as it hooks back over the bank, digesting.

From the trees near the banks I hear a song — "peter-peter-peter" — a tufted titmouse. The titmouse sings for two main reasons, to define his territory and to woo a mate. It's late in the season for the latter, so maybe he, like the heron, is letting me know I'm an intruder. This bird's song

is partly inside it, encoded, handed down from its parents
and their parents. Some species—herons and hawks and
ducks, for instance—will never expand their repertoire
beyond this genetic heritage, or if they do expand, it will
be by the nudge of accident. But for my titmouse, and for
most songbirds, their music is only partly in the genes. It is
also *learned*, which means it is varied and individual. This
is why a modern mockingbird can imitate a chainsaw or
car alarm. A bird's song, then, belongs both to their species
and themselves. Donald Kroodsma, the dean of avian vocal
behavior, writes: "Listen carefully to robins or individuals
of almost any songbird species as well, and you can hear
how each bird sings with his own voice by varying his songs
in either small or large ways from birds of his own kind."

My friends from my younger days laughed when they
found out I had gotten deeply into birds. *Birds*, of all things.
Fancy, pretty little birds. These friends were mostly athletes
and they saw me as an athlete, too, not to mention as someone who was gruff and crude and drank too much. And
now . . . birds!

What I might have said to them, if I'd had the nerve, was
that it was nothing fancy or pretentious that had led me to
birds. Quite the opposite in fact. I believe that birds held the
secret to something I'd been searching for. I slowly came to
understand that it had been *contact* I'd been after the whole
time, and that I had first sought out contact in drink and sport.
What I might have said was that the contact that I craved
was right there in an osprey's dive. But maybe it's best that I
kept quiet. They would have laughed back then, I'm sure.
But they are getting older now and it will not surprise me if
a few of them gradually find themselves turning to birds.

But still, the question: Why birds? I mentioned contact

but it goes beyond even that. I think the answer ultimately has something to do with both narcissism and its opposite. I go to birds selfishly but I also go to them because they are one of the few things that are capable of prying me out of myself. They don't do this always or even often and when they do it it's not for very long. But they do it. They give me transport along with contact. For that, and the fact that they fly, I love them. I don't like the geeky aspect of learning their names and calls as much as I like the sheer simplicity and transcendence of their lives. I am not talking about god here, and maybe god is not necessary. Maybe bird is enough.

At my worst moments I live trapped in what my old professor Walter Jackson Bate called "the subjective prison cell of self." I try to remember, during the dark, depressed, inward-turned times, that not only is there a world beyond me but that I have gone there — however briefly — and believe I will be able to go there again. This is the most reassuring thing I know. Not success or god or the big rock candy mountain. But the simple fact that there is still a world beyond us. That we are not alone.

Let's just assume for a minute that the experts are right and the world is doomed. Let's assume that when my four-year-old daughter is my age she will be living in a crowded slum apartment eating human-being patties like those in *Soylent Green*. What am I supposed to do about that? As I said above: I just don't fucking know.

And how much does my long-term doom affect what I will do on a day-to-day basis?

I will still drink my coffee; still make my things-to-do list; still go to work; still pick up my daughter at preschool;

still watch my birds. I might think about eco-doom once or twice a week but it won't truly impact my consciousness. When will that change?

Perhaps there will come a time when the problem is so pressing that we all rally around to fight. Perhaps we will pull an all-nighter and summon Bruce Willis and his crew of roughnecks and somehow save the world. But while this last is a story I would like to believe, a story I hope for, it isn't a story that I am going to put money on. Gloom and doom, while less palpable, seem a more likely forecast.

And this is just about where my brain usually freezes up again. This is where I always feel the need to take things down a few notches, to leave the problem behind for a while and turn to other concerns. Extreme fear — THE END OF THE WORLD! — leads to extreme thinking. Trembling before the world, we create apocalyptic scenarios and cast ourselves as prophets. Consider your own life: the way during a middle-of-the-night panic your thoughts spiral away from Earth, zigging and shooting and swirling upward. How to ground those thoughts? Where to root them?

I don't know about you, but my own inclination is to return to the personal, which is not to turn from the altruistic to the selfish. What I am suggesting is that, as pressing as the end of the world is, most of us have other fish to fry. I am not saying that this should be the case, just that it is. And I am not the first to suggest that, as vital as saving the world is, saving ourselves is of some importance, too.

$$\times$$

The dark secret of kayaking is that it can be pretty boring. Even with the stimulation of the changing weather and animal life, there are moments when the activity

grows tedious and my back and arms ache. Doing anything for eight hours will wear you down. On the other
hand the boring moments are more than counterbalanced
by the delightful ones. On the banks of the marsh I see
empty mussel shells and wonder if I'll catch a glimpse
of a river otter. *That* would be worth any tedium. Less
romantic than imagining that sight, but equally stimu-
lating, is the twenty minutes I spend paddling through
what signs announce as a LICENSED SHOOTING PRE-
SERVE. Gunfire tends to keep the human mind alert.

The noise dies out as the river seems to change to
creek. Suddenly I am twisting and turning back on myself in a sinuous maze, the marsh undermining any sense
of progress. It often feels like I am going backwards, but
I know that if I just keep paddling I'll cover the thirteen
miles I need to before I get to my campsite by nightfall.

As I slog through the marshy passage, red-winged blackbirds, proud of their blazing orange epaulets, cluck at me,
scolding. They let go with their three-word song, the last
note like a punchline. Calmer now, I return to the ideas that
spooked me an hour ago. It would be mauling a metaphor
to say that water grounds me, but at the very least all this
sweating and sun and full-on weather helps me consider
the prospect of our environmental annihilation without
risking another panic attack. I know I can offer no global
theories, but maybe I can do something more modest: offer
examples of people, like Dan, who have made nature—and
fighting for nature—part of their lives and seem the better for it. This may not be much help in the face of the
greater gloom and doom, but it's really all I've got.

I suspect that this is something like the way Dan felt
when his superiors first sent him off to work on the river,

almost as a prank. He must have been overwhelmed by the seemingly impossible problem of greening the Charles. Why impossible? Because the land he needed, if he were to re-plant the river's banks, had been owned or appropriated by individuals and corporations, and had been for decades. How could he possibly convince them that they should relinquish something they thought theirs? Did he glimpse right away that this would be his life's work, did he follow the vision from the start? No, it would have seemed pre-posterous. And if he had allowed himself to get excited, it would have led to excitement's opposite: panic and despair.

I wonder when it started to change for him. When did the fear and anxiety turn into something else? When did that frozen feeling in his brain begin to melt into momentum? Because, that is the thing about impossible tasks. Yes, they are intimidating; yes, they are daunting; yes, they can paralyze us. But they also can excite us, chal-lenge us, enlarge us. *What if I can really do this?* he must have thought at some point. Anyone who has tackled anything big — building a house, fighting a battle, writ-ing a book — knows the joy of the moment when the tide finally turns. And if the task is Quixotic, all the better. In his book, *Life Work,* the poet Donald Hall records the moment when he asked the sculptor Henry Moore what "the meaning of life" was. Moore replied: "The secret of life is to have a task, something you devote your entire life to, something you bring everything to, every minute of the day for your whole life. And the most important thing — it must be something you cannot possibly do!" Exactly! Perhaps there was even a point where Dan started to relish how absurd, how huge, the task at hand was.

Tell me to save the world and I will panic. Some jobs are simply too big, too daunting. Too much for one individual. But tell me to save a chunk of that world, a river say, and I might just become engaged. Give me something to work at, to work with, outside myself, and I will.

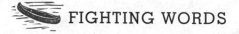 FIGHTING WORDS

I've always liked the word "turtle." Like "boing" or "scrotum" it seems innately comic. Today turtles, specifically painted turtles, are my companions; over the course of the afternoon I see hundreds of them. Almost despite myself, I'm getting to know their yellow and dark-green striped heads, the orange under their shells, the glistening water on those shells before they plop into the water. It's a beautiful sight, but let's face it: This marsh is not exactly pristine and in the black banks of muck I see tennis balls and beer bottles and, mysteriously, dozens of orange golf balls. When I finally emerge from the marsh, I pass a dock with a large American flag, unfurled for the coming holiday, and, next to the dock, a massive fire pit on the riverbank.

It isn't until mid-afternoon that I pass the first human being I've seen since leaving Dan this morning. This is an amazing fact considering I've been paddling through the suburban towns of Medfield, Millis, and Sherborn. It's a guy about my age fishing under a bridge. He claims to have caught eighteen fish—most recently a catfish and a bass. The Charles, I know, used to be a dead place. "Dirty Water," as the song went, so even the possibility that he has caught this many is reassuring. The guy asks me to look for a lure he lost downstream and I do after shouting goodbye.

Late in the afternoon I see another kayaker. Strangely though, rather than a feeling of companionship, I experience a prickly irritation, something maybe not too dissimilar

to the way the great blue heron feels upon seeing me. What
is this guy doing on *my* river? Of course I shout hello but
it might be more honest to emit a heron-like *sproak!* The
moment passes soon enough, though, and I am alone again.
I paddle below a railroad trestle, navigate a field of sunken
logs, and enter the Rocky Narrows Reservation, where I will
camp for the night. Rocky Narrows is conservation land,
owned and protected by the Trustees of Reservations.

I set up camp on a little ledge of grass a few feet above
the river. Here the water pivots around my campsite and the
little beach where I pull up the kayak. Nearby, a large willow
kneels, dipping its hair in the river. Once I feel organized,
I grab my pack and pull out a beer and a sandwich and sit
with my legs hanging over the ledge to drink my beer and
listen to the kissy noise of a chipmunk. A Baltimore oriole
flashes by.

After I finish the beer, I reach deep into my dry bag,
uneasy about the shameful task I have to perform next.
Dan and I have agreed that I will call him to fine tune the
morning's meeting, which means this is officially my first
camping trip armed with a cell phone. But when I pull the
phone out I discover that it is dead. Not just a little dead
either—there is nothing that says "No Service" or "Dead
Battery" or even "Alltell." No, this is utter death. I shake
it a little and push a few of the buttons in simian fashion
and then think about slamming it on a rock or something.
What follows is a strange moment of panic: egads, I'm
disconnected. I can feel my mind beginning to obsess over
the problem, and can imagine spending the next couple of
hours trying to resuscitate the machine. Not wanting to go
down that ugly route, I jam the phone back into the dry bag
and open a second beer. To my surprise, it doesn't take but

a minute to move beyond the phone crisis. So strange that even just turning off a cell phone, or being unintentionally disconnected from one, is a step into a wilder world.

I sip the beer and watch a long finger of light shaft down through the pines. It occurs to me that this would be a good spot to have sex if I were traveling with, say, my wife. I scribble down notes for an essay about wild sex in the wild—anything to help jazz up Nature's dowdy reputation. Meanwhile, streaks of sunset bleed into the river as a beaver plows by, heading back upstream. A barred owl lets out a series of classic whoos. Solo camping can be both thrilling and terrifying. I remember the first time I spent a couple nights alone in California's Lassen Park; I was sure the deer grazing outside the tent were killer bears. Over the years, I've become gradually less nervous. The woods behind me feel substantial and it seems I have the place to myself, at least until I hear a loud stomping and yelling coming down one of the paths. What enemy tribe is this? Three joggers and two dogs crash their way toward my campsite and suddenly my patch of wildness feels a little tamer. When they see my tent they grow quiet, and while they stop to let their dogs splash in the river I tell them about my trip. To my own surprise my voice sounds excited, almost overly so, and I realize I am already turning the day into a story.

I have always enjoyed spending days alone—solo days carry a special thrill—but for me, as a writer and storyteller and human animal, there is something else going on during these trips. I am readying my narrative, preparing to tell someone, itching to recreate my day. Pity the poor innocent who is the first person I bump into after these trips—the unlucky woman, for instance,

who sat next to me at the coffee shop counter in Chester
after my trip into Lassen—who gets her ear talked off.

I ask the runners how they happen to have come this
far into the woods, and learn that I'm not quite as secluded
as I hoped: there's a trailhead and a road a couple of miles
away. After they leave it quickly grows dark. I urinate
around the camp's perimeters to ward off other visitors and
return to my ledge over the water, waiting for the moon,
breathing in the slightly skunky smell of the river. I consider smoking the cigar I've stuffed in my dry pack, but
when the moon doesn't show up, I climb into my tent. The
night is quiet enough, despite the steady highway howl in
the background. I settle in my sleeping bag with a book
and flashlight.

I'm reading a book called *Break Through*, written by Ted
Nordhaus and Michael Shellenberger, two lifelong environmental advocates best known for releasing an attention-
grabbing essay called "The Death of Environmentalism."
That paper, which sparked a lively debate, advocated
breaking environmentalism out of its granola ghetto and
tackling global warming head-on, which, according to the
authors, and contrary to most conservatives, would actually create jobs and help the economy. I thought I'd pick
up the book because it seemed to fit my present mood,
and I'd heard that Nordhaus and Shellenberger, like me,
have grown tired of both musty mysticism and hysterical
apocalypse-ism, favoring a more practical, hard-headed
brand of environmentalism. I find myself nodding through
their initial arguments as the authors criticize yet another
manner of speaking about nature, that of the technocrat.

It gradually dawns on me, though, that the two authors seem to rail against the technocracy with their own form of techno-speak. I really wanted to like this book, but while I am full of admiration for these two men—mostly for their willingness to jab a stick in the environmental hornets' nest—as I read on it seems to me that they ultimately lack a truly creative response to crisis. They want "greatness," which they conveniently define as their own Apollo energy proposals. They tell me that what drives those of us interested in nature—which they consistently, ridiculously define as "hiking"—is a kind of post-materialist affluence, mocking anyone who might have more complex reasons to seek out the non-human world. Meanwhile, they happily belittle the contributions of old time environmental heroes like Rachel Carson. They seem to believe that human beings started to think about nature in the nineteenth century, around the same time Thoreau did, conveniently forgetting, or misplacing, the million years or so when we *lived* in the natural world.

In fact, what astounds me as I make my way through their text is that I don't encounter a single rock or tree or bird. Before too long I'm tempted to unzip the tent and toss the book in the river with the rest of the debris headed seaward. It's not that I disagree with a lot of their premises. Their willingness to criticize their august environmental forefathers, to suggest that the problems of poverty and environmentalism are deeply intertwined, is definitely praiseworthy. And whether or not you agree with them, their take is refreshing in that they try to shake things up. They also, for the most part, attempt to translate environmental policy into English while eschewing the gloomy rhetorical style that environmentalists have been known for

since the dark days of the seventies when Jimmy Carter
and his sweater first preached to us about conserving.

And yet the book is a hard slog. The authors constantly
stress the need for a larger "vision," using the word again
and again, but their own vision remains a little murky. Like
so many professional activists, they seem to suffer from
conservative think-tank envy, waxing poetic about the
Republicans' ability to appeal to our self-interest through
"core values," as if values were merely strategic and vision
merely a selling point. They suggest, for instance, that environmentalists focus more on "the job creation benefits of
things like retrofitting every home and building in America."
Well, retrofitting is nice, but it's not exactly a vision for
a livable future—maybe just a trip to Home Depot.

Then there's a larger problem: The authors tell us that
environmentalists don't acknowledge the potential of
human beings, and that they, on the other hand, hope to
free our great human potential. But their view of human
beings is cobbled together from a mish-mash of humanist
psychologists, neo-conservative critics, and what they keeps
stressing are the great breakthroughs of social psychology
over "the last fifty years," which seems a particularly arbi-
trary time period when considering human development.

What does it all add up to? They sell human beings way
short. They discount, for all their talk of vision, the power
of ideas. Take environmentalism, for instance: according
to the authors it came about in the sixties because we as a
society had become "post-material" and affluent, which led
to the great liberal agenda that environmentalism was part
of. They dismiss as antiquated and dusty anyone who buys
into the old mythos, anyone who dares believe that actual
thinkers and writers, like Rachel Carson, had an influence

on how people acted. Carson's story in fact is just the sort
of cobwebbed tale they think we must get rid of. They don't
exactly explain why this is so, nor do they rebut the impact
of her ideas on her times—how, for instance, Carson's book
led directly to the congressional hearings that led to the
banning of DDT and the founding of the Environmental
Protection Agency. No big deal, I guess. We are nonetheless
supposed to buy their premise, based on a crazy quilt of
sources, that environmentalism's flowering owed nothing
to ideas but was a mere sociological byproduct of wealth.

The most thought-provoking chapter in their book
considers Brazil, but it follows an argument that is deeply
confusing, and a bit disturbing. It goes a little like this:
Americans are really only concerned about the environment
because we are affluent and "post-materialist" (not because
human beings evolved in, and therefore probably have
some affinity for, nature) and other countries will only care
about the environment once they become post-material.
Therefore it is imperative that we, rather than in any way
try to restrain growth, encourage other nations, like Brazil,
to follow us down the post-materialist path. So how can
we help save the rainforest? Since only post-materialists can
care about the environment, we need to create economic
stimulus packages so that other countries become affluent, and post-material, and therefore are ready to save their
environment that—oops—will already have disappeared
in the process of their becoming post-material. They claim
we are hypocrites not to try and help others to have what
the United States has, but then again they acknowledge
that if others have what we have the world will be ruined.

Nordhaus and Shellenberger begin their book by citing
Martin Luther King, Jr.'s "I have a dream" speech, and end

by again claiming that what we need is vision. But Martin
Luther King, Jr.'s vision was a clear and passionate one:
All people should be treated equally and fairly. Here is
their dream, as I summarize it: *Countries should achieve an
abundance similar to the United States and gradually achieve
a post-materialism that will allow them, gradually, to get interested in environmentalism (and hiking).* Not quite as catchy as
King's, you must admit. It makes you wonder why they so
dislike the old dream—the one about "saving the world."

What most surprises me is how these two ever ended
up going into a field that had the word "environment" in
it. Their bios state that they have spent their entire careers
as part of, or advisers to, environmental organizations,
and you can't help but feel they would have benefited
from taking a few other jobs, maybe even one that got
them out of the office. It isn't just that they seem to have
little respect for the idealistic, passionate environmentalists who came before them, it's that I see no evidence at
all that either of these men, at any point in their lives,
have ever interacted with the nature that they so like to
theorize about. They seem to care little for the natural
world, except as it pertains to theories and models.

You'll have to forgive me, dear reader, for going on so
long about these two individually, but as I fume I realize
they are coming to embody for me much of what is wrong
with the environmental movement these days: primarily
the belief that humans are only data points; that theory and
policy will guide us beyond the troubled present we occupy
and the future it suggests. Policy and theory are great, but
they're only as strong as the belief of the people meant to
follow them. So Nordhaus and Shellenberger come in for
a beating here, but only because, to date, they're the best

effigies I've found yet for the environmental technocracy.
Sorry guys.

✕

I sleep pretty well on a cushion of pine duff and only get
up twice during the night. Once to piss and another time
when a loud noise jerks me out of sleep—just the commuter train rumbling past a couple of miles away, letting
off the shriek of its whistle. And then another noise, much
stranger, a noise that the train's whistle calls up. The train
initiates the dialogue, but the coyotes continue it eagerly.
They howl wildly for a good half hour after the train has
passed, their howling in turn setting off the distant yip-
ping and wailing of domestic dogs. The blurry dialogue
between what is wild and what is tame seems particularly
appropriate as a lullaby. I think back to when I lived in the
city this river is bound for, the year my daughter was born
and the year I tracked the coyotes that have made this their
urban territory, their tracks then tracing a path in the snow
along the frozen Charles, right down into the city's heart.

I listen to the chorus for a while, how long I don't
remember, before drifting back off to sleep.

✕

I wake to a river covered with mist. A blanket of white punc-
tuated by fingers of sunlight stretching down toward the
water as small whirlwinds of steam rise up to meet them.

Groggily, I return to last night's argument with
Nordhaus and Shellenberger. It turns out that they bug
me as much in daylight as after dark. These two claim to
dislike scoldings, but their book sure feels like one. After
reading for awhile, I prowl my small patch of shoreline. I

feel chastised and it isn't chastisement that we need. We need the opposite. We need language—simple, plain, impassioned—that can be used both to describe our love for nature and to rally humans, actual people living in the *world*, to the fight to save it. A language that calls us away from computers, think tanks, and ethereal theories so that we may return to the ground truths of the places we call home. Why talk about language again, you ask, when there are polar bears to save? Because language comes first, the source, the rallying cry before the fight.

One thing I do enjoy in Nordhaus and Shellenberger's book is their fondness for Winston Churchill. The biographer William Manchester wrote of Churchill's speeches during World War II: "Another politician might have told them: 'Our policy is to continue the struggle; all our focus and resources will be mobilized.'"[4] Instead Churchill's words rose to the occasion and he spoke directly of sacrifice, of "blood, toil, tears, and sweat."[5] If we are indeed entering a time of crisis—and everyone tells us we are—then we will need the direct and urgent language of crisis, a language that fills us with hope, despite the darkness.

Part of what a living language must do is address the crisis itself, but more importantly it must tackle the psychology of environmentalism. How do we go from engaging in a full-on panic attack to taking small steps, from listless apathy to the beginnings of action on a wide and wild scale? For me those questions spring from this one: Why save a world you don't care about? After all, how do we fight for something that is no longer a part of our lives? Or to put it another way, how do we start to care for something we have nothing to do with? Beyond buying into the faddish popularity of

our new all-green, all-natural, consumerism, the majority of people in this country have little to no contact
with the natural world in their daily lives. What this
new language must do, in clearly unsentimental terms,
is to cultivate a return to, a love and delight for, wildness. Because that is what we are losing when we lose
daily contact with birds, animals, trees, water, and land.
Part of the problem, of course, is what I would call the
nature calendar view of nature: over there is spectacular untrammeled NATURE and then there's what we've
got. But I am here to say that what we've got, right here,
trammeled and all, ain't so bad. We simply need to fall
in love with what is left, with the limited wildness that
remains. That is what Dan Driscoll did with the river
I'm staring out at now. He saw past the piles of Coors
Light cans and shopping carts floating in the water and
fell for the coyotes, the hills, and the black crowned night
herons that had come back to nest along the shore.

My own experience suggests that love, and sometimes
hate, are much better motivators than theory. For several
years — the most intense years of my life in many ways — I
lived on a deserted beach on Cape Cod, squatting in the
homes of the wealthy during the off-season, and during that
time I fell hard for one particular section of rocky beach.

I didn't clearly recognize it at the time but that period
was a love affair. And then the love affair was interrupted
when, one day, someone began constructing a trophy home
on the bluff. I was filled with something close to rage, and
for the first time in my life, found myself attending town
meetings and writing letters of protest. I bring this last
point up, not to boast of any strain of righteousness, but
because I believe it speaks to what motivates many of us

to act. The writer Jack Turner puts it well: "To reverse this situation we must become so intimate with wild animals, with plants and places, that we answer to their destruction from the gut. Like when we discover the landlady strangling our cat."[6] Our greatest environmentalists, Teddy Roosevelt and John Muir among them, were instinctive fighters, who also happened to spend plenty of time outdoors. More of us need to follow their lead. It is not my place to offer pep talks, aphorisms, or dictums. But if I had to give one piece of practical advice it would be this: Find something that you love that they're fucking with and then fight for it. If everyone did that—imagine the difference.

If environmental psychology is my topic, some of the pressing questions are: What allows a person to go beyond paying lip service to nature and to actually live with it in this modern, muddled world? How can we fall in love with something so limited and wounded? And how can we go from loving to fighting? Finally, we must consider what role, if any, that hope plays in these questions.

A while back I read an essay by a writer named Derrick Jensen, in which he argued for a politics of hopelessness. I couldn't disagree more. Without hope and the energy it provides we curl into the mental equivalent of the fetal position, hiding from the world. "Where there is no hope, there can be no endeavor," wrote Samuel Johnson.[7] He was not talking about the Disney variant of hope, but the real animal. It's the light that filters down into our dark brains, sparking our neurons. The brightening after darkness, which energizes like the quickening of the world in spring. A thawing and movement into activity, an activity that then gains momentum. This is hope as a physical thing: The hope that spring inspires, after the long winter.

It is just this sort of hope that energizes me now as I pace this bank, hope spiced, of course, with a dash or two of vitriol. A fine cocktail. It occurs to me to write a manifesto, but one quite different from Nordhaus and Shellenberger's. My agenda is simple: To describe the ways that my own life, and the lives of some people I admire, are connected to the natural world, and the benefits that come from that connection, benefits that are not always obvious. To provide a way for those of us who would blanch at calling ourselves environmentalists to begin to at least think of ourselves as *fighters*, in the way that citizens suddenly think of themselves as soldiers during times of war. Finally, by both argument and example, to provide a new language for those of us who care about nature.

II. A LIMITED WILD

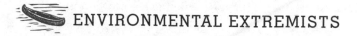# ENVIRONMENTAL EXTREMISTS

Rags of mist drift above the river. Despite the usual hassle of breaking camp, and sore arms from the day before, I feel good this morning. Part of that is the simple pleasure of being on the river, and part is the "phew" element that accompanies any morning after a night of solo camping. As in, "Phew, I wasn't killed by bears," or, in this case, joggers or coyotes. I stuff my clothes and gear into their appropriate bags, pack the kayak, and I am back on the water. The sun greets me around the first bend, burning off the mist, and around the next I look back at the chalky outline of a nearly full moon.

Though my cell phone is dead, I trust Dan has figured that out, and I assume that we will meet, as planned, just a quarter mile downstream at Bridge Street in the town of Dover. I look forward to seeing Dan, and to turning this solo journey into a group adventure, but moreover I look forward to something that Dan's wife Donna has promised to bring: coffee.

I met Donna, and the Driscolls' son Dylan, in Wellfleet when I picked up the kayaks. Dylan was a delightfully rambunctious two-year-old who instantly made me homesick for my four-year-old daughter, Hadley. Donna I was less sure about at first.

"I'm here to make a hero of your husband!" I said to break the ice. I expected something either supportive or sardonic in return but instead she said simply, "Well, someone

should do it." She seemed similarly distant as Dan and I
sat on his porch poring over maps to plan our trip. I guess
I understood that while I was offering Dan adventure, all
I was offering her was a couple of days as a single parent.
The only moment she perked up was when I mentioned
that I was enlisting a friend of mine, a kayak guide, to be
our "Sherpa," making sure the kayaks and cars were all in
the right place, and helping supply us with food and drink
along the way. It turned out that this was something that
she would be interested in doing—for a price. Wanting to
please Dan, and his family, I instantly said yes, not really
thinking through the possible challenges of a wife serving as
a husband's gofer. When I handed her the "Sherpa list" with
her duties on it, the word COFFEE had been printed neatly
at the top in all capitals.

There are no signs of the Driscolls at the launch, but
my cell phone was also my only clock, so I'm not sure if it's
yet close to the eight-thirty meeting time we agreed upon.
I paddle a half-mile downstream between heavily wooded
banks to the Broadmoor Wildlife Sanctuary, searching the
branches for birds. I see a tanager blaze by, its chest the
color of blood, and add it to an already impressive list of
species I've noted over the previous twenty-four hours.
This is no accident: The river is a magnet for both residential and migrating birds. As suburbs cover more and more
previously undeveloped space, the few remaining islands of
undisturbed land, like the Broadmoor with its lands patched
together by Massachusetts Audubon from purchases of private land beginning in 1962, become even more vital—not
just as year-round habitat but also as reliable pit stops during
migrations.

After a while, I double back to the launch site but there

is still no sign of Dan. I pull the kayak and listen to com-
muters bomb down the little road, kicking up dirt. After
another half hour, an old station wagon with a canoe
lashed to the top careens off the road and into the parking
lot and the entire Driscoll family tumbles out. The family mood can best be described as frazzled, if not agitated.
Something tense is passing between Dan and Donna. (It
isn't hard to imagine that waking the whole family at six
so that Dad can go canoeing might not be the most popular idea.) They apologize for their tardiness and I excit-
edly describe the death of my cell phone. I am completely
ignored as a minor marital skirmish ensues about whether
or not Dylan should be allowed to wade in the water (which
he is already doing). While that is going on, I peek, with
dying hope, in the car's windows to see if there are any
cups in the cup-holders. Just then Donna walks up behind.

"I'm sorry we were running late," she says flatly. "We
didn't have time to get coffee."

"That's fine," I say with a big smile.

I want to kill her.

While I contemplate the gloomy prospect of a decaf-
feinated morning, Dan inspects the banged up bottom of
the kayak, slowly shaking his head. But neither of us is in
the mood to dwell on the negative, not when it's morning and we have a day on the river in front of us. Soon
the bustling momentum of preparation takes over: getting the canoe down off the car rack, throwing the kayak
back up, packing the canoe, looking at the map to plan
out our next meeting point with Donna. She rejects our
first suggested rendezvous, which confirms what I already
suspect: She will be a decidedly un-Sherpa-like Sherpa. I
think of my friend Ian, who was my first choice for the

job. He is a childhood pal, an outdoorsman, as devoted
as a puppy, and, had nepotism not reared its ugly head,
he would have embraced being part of the adventure
with the sort of goofy enthusiasm the job requires.

Lack of caffeine, no doubt, is darkening my thoughts,
and as we push out onto the river I wonder if an early beer
might alleviate the inevitable headache.

It turns out that I don't need the beer, or the coffee, at
least not right away, since the river itself, and the exercise
of paddling on it, will soon enough serve to lift my mood.

Dan has a different avenue toward transcendence:
No sooner have we paddled around the first bend and, in
Thoureauvian fashion, left family behind, when he an-
nounces that it's "time for a little eye opener." With that
he whips out something that smells of skunk, and lights
a bowl. This is where Dan parts ways with Thoreau, who
preferred "the natural sky to an opium-eater's heaven."

"You can thank Ronald Reagan for this," he says. "Thanks
to his drug laws we started growing the best bud in the
world right at home."

He offers the bowl. I have plenty of friends like Dan—
doctors, lawyers, stockbrokers, competent professionals
all—who seem capable of using pot as mild relaxant. That's
great for them, I suppose, but my system is a little different.
One puff for me and our idyllic paddle would transform
into a Conrad-like journey into the heart of paranoia. I
politely decline.

$$\times$$

We paddle quietly for a while on the green shadowy river,
and then, as if on cue, a young deer, tawny and hesitant,
emerges from the woods, freezing when it sees us. It is a

stunning sight there by the bank, and we lift our paddles and let the current carry us, trying to stay as still as the animal. Once we round the next bend we laugh and hoot at our good luck.

"You see, that wouldn't have happened if we weren't attuned with the river," Dan says.

I nod, though I'm not so sure. The deer was pretty easy to see. But I'm not about to argue. I listen as Dan launches into the first of the morning's monologues.

"Nature is my religion," he begins. "Pantheism is my religion!"

He talks in this vein for a while, and then his sentences take what I will begin to recognize as a characteristic turn. He can't really talk about his love of nature without spouting a lot of semi-mystical mumbo jumbo. I know how it is. But when his words start snaking their way to the topics of activism and politics they become bold and original.

"We nature lovers are hypocrites, of course," he says. "We are all hypocrites. None of us are consistent. The problem is that we let that fact stop us. We worry that if we fight for nature, people will say, 'But you drive a car,' or, 'You fly a lot,' or, 'You're a consumer, too.' And that stops us in our tracks. It's almost as if admitting that they are hypocrites lets people off the hook."

I pull my paddle out of the water to listen.

"What we need are *more* hypocrites," he said. "We need hypocrites who aren't afraid of admitting it but will still fight for the environment. We don't need some sort of pure movement run by pure people. We need hypocrites!"

I think of Edward Abbey fighting for the West while throwing empty beer cans out the window of his truck. I think of my own environmental Achilles heel, a dainty

preference for hot baths over showers—not nearly as cool
as Abbey's boozing, but possibly as wasteful. And then I
think of everyone I know and know of and can't come up
with anyone who has an entirely clean eco-slate. Which
seems to mean that, logically, Dan is right: If only non-
hypocrites are going to fight for the environment then it
will be an army of none.

When Dan finishes talking we turn our attention
more fully to the work of paddling. We have a good ways
to go, almost sixteen miles, if we are going to make it to
our destination, the less-than-romantically-named Long
Ditch, by sunset. As we glide through the Broadmoor a
sharp-shinned hawk banks over the river and lands in a
tree, spreading its tail like a delicate oriental fan. Around
the next bend, a statue of a praying woman stands on a
low triangular rock on the river bank, her face mottled by
the shadows of oak leaves. Dan mentions that we are in
Natick, and that praying, of the enforced variety, has a long
history here. The state mandated the creation of Native
American towns for the Massachusetts tribe in this area,
evidently to help them preserve their culture—except for
that one minor cultural component: their religion. These
were Christian towns, the inhabitants referred to as "the
Praying Indians." Now Natick is a mostly white suburb,
though not quite as affluent as some of the surrounding towns. It is also, Dan tells me, one of the few spots
along the river where the same town forms both banks.

"Almost everywhere else the river is the border between
towns," he says. "You can look at it either way. As a connector or a separator. Either way we are almost always paddling
down the middle of a border between towns."

Before lunch we portage around the South Natick Dam

and float through the backyards of Wellesley's stately mansions. The river seems to like the easy affluence; arcing in and out of Wellesley in a lazy oxbow. This is a town where sixty-six percent of the households have at least one advanced degree, and it's one of the last, long stretches of river before we hit more urban and dam-filled waters. We paddle hard for an hour, cutting a line between Needham and Dover. On my map I count fourteen dams, though I have read somewhere that there are at least twenty.

Our next dam portage is the Cochrane. While South Natick required nothing more than sliding the canoe over a hill of dirt and pine needles, this dam presents more of a challenge. We finally take the boat out close to where the falls go over the dam, climb a hill covered with poison ivy, and muscle the canoe up onto a stone wall. Then we carry the canoe down Mill Street in Dover for about a hundred feet. There is no sidewalk, and cars seem to be taking the blind corner we are walking into at about two hundred miles an hour, so as soon as we hit the woods below the dam we cut back in, despite the fact that this requires more bushwhacking though poison ivy. Once the canoe is back in the river we scrub ourselves with sand and water, and hope we don't start itching soon.

As we paddle through the afternoon, I chew over what Dan said about hypocrisy.

Much has been made, of course, of the fact that celebrity environmentalists like Gore, McKibben, or even DiCaprio jet around the world to deliver their speeches about burning less fuel, and, on a much smaller scale, I'm the same sort of hypocrite. Over the last couple of months I have been flying all over the country, from sea to shining sea, burning massive amounts of fossil fuel as I preach, in part, about burning less fossil fuel. Call me Son of Gore.

I've been feeling a little bad about this but there is something freeing about Dan's admission that we are all, to some extent, full of shit. The larger point that he is making, and that I couldn't agree with more, is that none of us are pure, none clean.

It occurs to me that, in its frankness and open humor, this attitude could do the environmental movement a world of good. We need to start again, I'm convinced, and we might do that by admitting that we are limited, human animals, not idealistic, über creatures. This may seem obvious enough, and I certainly would have thought it so, but over the last few months, as I've traveled, I have come in contact with a certain type of environmentalist that I once thought was merely the bogeymen of far-right conservative imaginations. I once regarded "environmental extremists" the way I did the Loch Ness monster or Bigfoot, but it turns out *they are real*.

My first encounter came when I agreed to be on a scholarly panel with the writer I mentioned earlier, Derrick Jensen. A couple of weeks before the panel I sent out a friendly e-mail to the other panelists, suggesting we bounce some ideas off each other. Here is a sampling from the e-mail I got in response from him:

> You ask me what I think about so-called nature writing? I think the same about it that I think about any beautiful writing. There is no time for it. There is time for only one thing: *saving the earth*.

The world is being slaughtered and we need to
stop it. At this point writing is beside the point: the
only — and I mean *only* — thing that matters is to
stop this culture from killing the planet. The reason I feel comfortable saying that it's the only end
that matters is that without a landbase you don't
have anything. Everything — including beautiful
writing — emerges from and is secondary to the land.

The other writers and I felt a little cowed by the note,
embarrassed that we had been up to then correspond-
ing about such minor concerns as semicolons, tree frogs,
and imagery. We worried that we were poseurs next to
Derrick, that we should immediately *do* something, maybe
burn our bras or draft cards. I read his e-mail to a friend, a
writer who is much more careful about keeping his politics out of his essays than I am. He told me a story about
a Marxist poet who accosted Robert Frost and said: "No
poetry is worth its name unless it moves people to action." Frost replied: "I agree. The question is, *how soon?*"
   I admired Jensen's passion, and realized that, face-to-
face, we might have more in common than not. The sheer
earnestness of environmentalism can make me uneasy,
but force me to choose between a tad too much earnestness and melting ice caps and I'll take earnestness every
time. Still, something about his tone unsettled me. I was
reminded of one of my oldest friends, a man who not
long ago became obsessed with the theory of peak oil.
   Peak oil is the idea that we have already passed the high
point of petroleum production and will run out much
faster than most predict, bringing the world as we know
it grinding to a halt in the near future. It certainly could

be true, but it is far from a certainty. My problem is that
this old friend, who is otherwise a very nice guy, has let it
take over his life. Everything—his friends, his family, his
job—is now seen through the lens of peak oil. His marriage, for instance, has dissolved, in part because he was
critical of his wife for being concerned with quotidian
things like playing tennis and going out to dinner. How
could she care about such petty concerns when the world
was about to end? Lately he started talking about taking his kids up to the mountains with other like-minded
peak oil-ists where they will grow and can their own
food. Despite my own environmental leanings, I can't
help but feel that this plan has a Unabomber whiff to it.

I first learned how serious things had gotten when he
told me we "needed to talk." He is not a big talker, so I
knew something was up. After a bunch of "um"s and "ah"s,
he finally got to his point. A couple years before he and his
wife had asked my wife and I to be the legal guardians of
their children should anything happen to them. But now he
was having second thoughts. When I asked why, he *um*-ed
and *ah*-ed some more before mumbling something that I
had to ask him to repeat.

"I'm not sure you're going to make it," he said.

"Make it?"

"In the coming times."

Then, by way of explanation, he added: "You and your
wife know nothing about canning food."

All I could do was shake my head. Not so much at the
silliness of what he said as at the tone, the sheer certainty
with which he said it. I, too, believe that the next centuries
will bring some radical changes and that out of necessity
our worlds, and food, will become more local. But still, I

couldn't help but feel that he had become a Dickens character, consumed by his ONE IDEA while forgetting anything
that fell outside that theory: friends, say, or common sense,
or his wife.

I've been thinking about my old friend as I wrestle with
my own desire to fight for the environment, while still
fighting against calling myself an "environmentalist."

Maybe this resistance springs from my ingrained sus
picion of being part of anything organized (especially
now that it's popular). This urge to resist labels might not
have any larger repercussions, but then again it might.
I think it may come from a fear of seeing the world too
simply, of falling into the trap of believing there *is* just
one answer, one way, one thing, one solution. And perhaps it is the larger fear of creating a too-simple map
of the world in a time when the world could not possibly be more complex, messy, and interconnected.

Or maybe I'm just afraid? "The earth is our home,"
the writer Edward Abbey said simply enough, "And we
must protect our home." So what do I say to that? Well, in
response I lean on another writer, a writer who was Abbey's
contemporary, but who fought an entirely different fight.
I think of James Baldwin's lines on racism near the end of
one of the finest modern essays, "Notes of a Native Son":

> It began to seem that one would have to hold in
> the mind forever two ideas which seemed to be in
> opposition. The first idea was acceptance, the ac-
> ceptance, totally without rancor, of life as it is, and
> men as they are: in light of this idea, it goes without
> saying that injustice is a commonplace. But this did
> not mean that one could be complacent, for the

second idea was of equal power: that one must never, in one's own life, accept these injustices as commonplace but must fight them with all one's strength.

That gets at it best, better than Abbey's blunt passion. The complexity of the challenge, the need to, in Keats' words, "be in uncertainties." While I want to fight for a green world, I don't want to live my one life on earth as a caricature, a person who sees everything through one lens. It's when environmentalism becomes fundamentalism that I get nervous.

I feel the need to embrace opposites: to understand, on one hand, that life is sloppy, complicated, even ridiculous, and that destroying ourselves may be a fit ending to this farce; but to understand that, on the other hand, we need to fight with all our hearts to preserve what is left of this beautiful mess for our children and grandchildren.

So both ideas, which are, like Baldwin's, "in opposition," must be held in mind.

Which is not an easy thing to do.

Which may be why so few of us do it.

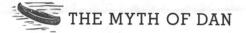 THE MYTH OF DAN

Obviously I see Dan—hearty, energetic, slightly crazy
Dan—as a counterbalance to the Derrick Jensen school
of environmentalism. But there's also something about
Dan's personal history that strikes me as typical, and possibly archetypical, of environmental fighters. As we paddle
down the river Dan fills in more details about that history.

"I was raised in Newton," he says. "My father eventually ended up as president of Payne Elevator, but he did
this with just a high school degree. He started out working class and he was always no-nonsense. I grew up as a
kind of punk without any environmental conscience. The
thing that changed my world was when my father bought a
house in Wellfleet. For years a friend of his from his bowl-
ing league tried to get him to buy this place. 'Where the
hell is Wellfleet?' my father said. But this friend talked about
how cheap the house was, and the joy of getting down
to Cape Cod in the summer. My father just said 'I have a
house already.' Finally, one day, over a few drinks, the guy
wore him down. My dad ended up agreeing to buy the
house, sight unseen, for 9,500 dollars. When he got home
and told my mother she threw a fit. 'Are you crazy?' she
yelled. Then she said the same thing my dad did. 'Why do
we need a house in *Wellesley*? We already have a house.'"

Cape Cod stirs up associations of tennis courts and
yacht clubs, and, more recently, of oversized trophy
houses, but the Cape of that time, the sixties, was still

the destination for many Massachusetts families, not just the rich. The father's purchase, an impulse buy after years of restraint, would change the course of his third child's life. Dan began spending summers in Wellfleet, and that, by his own account, transformed him.

"My father didn't have an environmental bone in his body, but suddenly I was spending time at a place that had marshes right out the back door. Whole days mucking around out on the marsh digging steamers and mussels and oysters. Some nights I fed our family from the marsh and I started a small business selling shellfish to neighbors. Something in me changed out there. I think in a lot of ways Wellfleet was the catalyst for the work I've done on the river. If I—through my love of the marshes on Cape Cod—could be transformed into someone with an eco-conscience then so could others. I thought, 'Well let's create other places for kids who maybe aren't lucky enough to go to the Cape. Let's give them some nature right at home.' And that's a lot of what drives me to create these wild places for kids to interact with nature."

"How did you start working for the state?" I ask him.

"Well I had been kicking around from job to job in my twenties. I was finally about to begin something real. I was going to start a nursery on Cape Cod. I had all the money together and everything. Then I drove down to Wellfleet and stayed up all night thinking. I thought about what that place meant to me and what I really wanted to do with my life. The next day I drove back to the University of Vermont, where I'd gone to school, and talked to my old professors. They told me I could start getting extension school credits toward a master's in natural resources planning.

"My father said, 'Don't do it. You're running away. You're not facing the world.'"

Left unsaid is that his father was dead wrong: This was exactly how Dan eventually faced the world. In fact, his rebellion from his father is an essential aspect of what I am coming to call, in my head, The Myth of Dan. Gary Snyder wrote that the West is a country of "men re- moved from the father image." Substitute "wilderness" for West and you can broaden the meaning. Theodore Roosevelt, to name our greatest presidential conserva- tionist, knew this first hand from his pilgrimages to the Badlands, the place that transformed him from a soft New York Daddy's boy into something harder and wilder.

The Myth of Dan goes something like this: as a child, the Dan Figure (as we will call him) discovers something in na- ture, something he will lose along the way. Later, as a young man, he wanders aimlessly before returning to that child- hood place away from society, into nature, a place of solitude, where he forms his vision. Part of this retreat involves a break from the parents. But retreat is not the end of it. Equally important is what the Dan Figure brings back from his re- treat. He must return with something—a vision, a book, an idea   and then he must present that thing to the world.

So the short version is: Dan finds nature as child, Dan wanders lost, Dan breaks from his father, Dan retreats to nature, Dan returns to the world. . . .

Let me add that I am aware that one of the reasons that I am attracted to Dan's myth is narcissistic: His quest bears more than a little resemblance to The Myth of Dave. I wouldn't be on this river at all if I hadn't made the odd decision, after graduating from college, of heading, not to law school or Wall Street, but to a town not far from Dan's stomping grounds on Cape Cod. I had only known that peninsula in the summers and decided, during my first year on my own, to live there in the off-season. I don't remember

how long it took me to realize that I had done a miraculous thing by moving to the Cape in September. The year
startled me. The wind swept out the clinging heat and the
tourists, and ushered in that clarifying light that made each
and every object—each blade of eel grass or cormorant
on a rock or outline of the gibbous moon—look like the
only thing left on earth. I watched the leafy world redden,
the sumac and poison ivy bloodying the bluffs right around
the time of the cranberry harvest. I laughed as thousands
of swallows gathered in groups, staging before their trip
south, and speckle-bellied starlings lined the phone wires,
and for the first time I began to learn the names of birds.
Also, I began my first book and became more confident
in my seemingly delusional decision to become a writer.
Looking back, I sometimes feel that from that moment
onward all my choices somehow spring from that first wild
fall. Obviously my life did not begin at twenty-three, and
the roots of what I did go back much further. But so much,
for me, hinged on my decision not to advance but to retreat.

Since I'm telling the story of two Massachusetts boys,
why not throw in a third? One reason so many of us turn
to Thoreau, other than his great sentences, is that the al-
legory of his life provides the template for almost all who
either write about, fight for, or simply love being in nature.
Think of it as a deeper, much-bolstered Myth of Dan. In
Thoreau's case we have a profound childhood attachment
to nature, to home, to Concord, followed by the adult
wanderer who is perceived as lost, a town handyman, a
Harvard graduate turned n'er-do-well who doesn't embrace
a real career, who has to answer the skeptical questions
of his fellow townspeople. And think of the many levels
on which Thoreau rejected the father: not only the mores

of the Puritan community or the town's patriarchy, but ultimately also those of his literary father, Emerson. Cynics like to mention that while at Walden Thoreau sometimes went home to eat at Mom's on Sundays, but he broke away from the family in much deeper and more profound ways. Emerson couldn't quite make sense of it, and that was partly because, in going to Walden, Thoreau practiced what Emerson preached. In spending his years by the pond, Thoreau lived out what has become the archetype of retreat. Finally, of course, there was what he brought back to the world: his resplendent, funny, and difficult book.

While the myth of retreat and return certainly isn't the only model, it's amazing how many who came after Thoreau played out variations on the theme. John Muir did so in bold, primary colors, famously and dramatically rejecting his abusive Calvinist father before leaving the farm to set out on his epic jaunts across the country, seeking out the wildest places. The theme plays out with more recent environmentalist heroes as well, with David Brower climbing his many mountaintops, and the members of Earth First!, led by Dave Foreman, retreating deep into the Sonoran Desert before emerging with a new and radical concept of what it means to be environmental.

Of course the word "retreat" takes on a whole new meaning in a time of war. There is the implication of running away. But one thing I find fascinating is how often retreat ultimately leads to its opposite: a political impact on the world. Again Thoreau serves as the most obvious and famous example, sending ripples from Walden Pond outward to, among other places, India and the American South, with both Gandhi and Martin Luther King, Jr. acknowledging Thoreau as a main, if not *the* main, influence on their work. More recently there's Rachel Carson, who, by retreating to the Maine coast to closely observe her tidal pools and eel grass, gave us a book that led to some of the most significant environmental changes of the last century. Carson reminds us again of the necessity of retreat, and puts the lie to the more cowardly definitions of the word. She shows us that, by continuing to return to our most private places, we can deeply engage the world.

✕

It's important to emphasize one central truth in all of these myths: a deep love for specific landscapes. For Dan it all began out there roaming the marshes. When we are young we naturally seek out secret places: we build forts, find shortcuts through the woods, climb trees. This is not environmentalism but instinct. As it turns out, trying to teach kids a strictly "environmental" curriculum often backfires. As the writer and educator David Sobel points out in *Beyond Ecophobia*, children who are taught that the natural world is being destroyed, that the rain forests are being mown down, and that a boogeyman called global warming is coming, often withdraw and distance themselves from nature. In fact there's no surer way to send them running for the TV or computer screen. Just as with other forms of abuse, children are hardwired to hide from abusive relationships with the world. It is better to simply introduce young children to nature by allowing them to *play* in the wild world.

Sobel writes of those formative years: "This is the time to immerse children in the stuff of the physical and natural worlds. Constructing forts, creating small imaginary worlds, hunting and gathering, searching for treasures, following streams and pathways, making maps, taking care of animals,

gardening and shaping the earth are perfect activities during this stage." Eventually, of course, they will learn about
the death of the rain forests, but first comes a more direct,
and playful, connection with the so-called environment.

We have lost something vital when we forget how to
build forts in our backyard. While most of us have matured
beyond our eleven-year-old selves, a similar logic of how we
care applies to adults.

"How do you connect young people to nature?" I asked
Dan before we portaged below the Cochrane Dam.

"Seriously?"

He thought about it for a minute.

"Mushrooms," he said finally. "I don't know if it's possible without doing mushrooms."

We laughed. This was a slightly different take on environmental education than David Sobel's. Of course Dan
was joking . . . or at least I thought he was.

But, joking or not, I took his larger point.

It doesn't start with prescriptions; it doesn't start with
shoulds; it doesn't start with finger wagging. It starts with fun,
it starts with building forts in our backyards, it starts with
animal explorations. And, it goes without saying—whether
you have a taste for hallucinogens or not—it starts with joy
and wildness. And it should never end.

Maybe, instead of building wonky policy initiatives,
Nordhaus and Shellenberger should take some time off to
build a tree fort.

 A LARGER FIGHT

Below Cochrane Dam is a mile or so of river that my map designates as "whitewater." That term might be a stretch, but for a beginning canoeist like me the fast water proves a challenge. Dan, more accomplished in a canoe, maneuvers the boat while my main job is to look for submerged rocks. I take this job seriously and it is exhilarating to be on alert, to call out to Dan when I see something, as he briskly steers the boat through the rocks. We are getting pretty good at it, a fairly competent team, but then, feeling cocky perhaps, we almost wreck the canoe on a sewer conduit.

The pipe, about five feet around, runs directly across the river, creating a three-foot mini-falls. We know we should get out of the boat instead of going over it, but we are both sick of portaging, and in truth it looks no more formidable than a speed bump. We circle above, sussing out ways to approach it, and then Dan opens the door, "What do you think?"

"Let's go for it." He nods and we paddle hard, I guess imagining that we will somehow be the first two people in the world to "jump" a canoe, leap the pipe, and heroically crash down below with the falls.

It doesn't quite work out that way. The canoe makes it almost exactly halfway over the pipe before we are stopped cold. The boat is transformed into a seesaw: my end is up, Dan's down. But then the seesaw concept gives way and suddenly my end is down, too, without Dan's going up. In other words, the canoe is cracking in half. The boat moans and buckles.

Far too slow and too late we jump out into hip-deep water and wrestle the cracked canoe to shore. Water rushes in through the crack as we drag the boat up the bank, where Dan immediately sets to repairing the damage with duct tape. While he works, he talks about all the great times he's had in that canoe over the years, the way you would talk about a friend at a funeral. I worry our spasm of exuberance has doomed the trip, but as Dan works his mood gradually lifts and it turns out the boat isn't quite dead yet. Lacking fiberglass, Dan jams a sandal into the crack and duct tapes it into place. Good as new. A half hour later we are back on the river, the canoe leaky now and ankle deep with muddy river water, but functional.

When water starts pouring in faster around the jammed sandal, I call back to Dan.

"What should we do?" I yell.

He thinks for a minute.

"Paddle as fast as you possibly can," he yells back.

Let's leave Dan and me paddling down the river for a minute.

I didn't want to rant at you in this book, though I've already failed. Like you, I often tune out or roll my eyes when my friends — particularly my less imaginative and more dogmatic friends — begin to talk politics. But I don't want this to be just another pretty little nature book with pretty little moments. I don't want to comfort you until you simply sigh *"ahah"* at the heron winging out over the river. I want to avoid giving you the payoff of a quiet lifting, a subtle glimpse into another, deeper, soul-stroking, natural way of being.

I want to shake you up, grab you by the lapels, take you to the woodshed, all that. I want to challenge you—to suggest that there is more to "living green" than recycling your cans or screwing in those damned light bulbs. I want to ask you to take seriously the proposition that many pay lip service to: The proposition that you are an animal living on a crowded planet with other animals and that, as such, you need to take some responsibility for being, what Emerson called, "a good animal."[8] I want to talk about the way that nature fits into this proposition, and not the nature one reads about but the nature I know, which is a good place for laughter, drinking, fires, and pine-duff-prickled sex. This version of nature is not technical or pseudo-groovy, and it certainly isn't a place where every waking moment is spent inside a panic attack about THE END OF THE WORLD.

Maybe, however, you are seeing some flaws in my argument. You will rightly say that Dan Driscoll's battle, and my battle with my neighbor on the Cape Cod bluff, are small, local fights. How do these relatively simple crusades stand up against enormous and complex problems like global warming, with that daunting adjective in its name, an adjective that emphasizes just how un-local the fight is? And though global warming has been presented as THE problem (when's the last time you heard warnings about nuclear winter?) there are dozens of global problems that range from species extinction to the food crisis, all of them substantially tougher than writing an angry letter to a trophy-home-building neighbor or planting some shrubs along the banks of a river. Ultimately, what do the little fights have to do with this larger fight?

Bill McKibben is someone who has made those larger issues, particularly global warming, his own personal fight, someone who has fought longer and harder—my

apologies to Al Gore and his Oscar—than anyone else in
the climate change ring. I've known him since we worked
on our college newspaper together; he was the editor-in-
chief and I the political cartoonist—positions that probably say worlds about our differences in temperament.[9]
In the years since college, McKibben has become the
leading environmental writer of our generation; a status
he has earned honestly by writing milestone books like
The End of Nature, which detailed the dangers of global
warming, twenty years before it was chic to do so.

Recently I read one of his newer books, *Deep
Economy*—a sort-of treatise on how we need to transform
our economy to meet the challenges of the future—and
was, as you can imagine, strongly predisposed to liking
it, and, in fact, did. It seemed to me a tight summation
of where we need to go: away from our obsession with
growth at all costs, toward a dependence on local economies, and obviously away from slurping down oil and gobbling resources like a bunch of drunken gluttons at a feast.
Hovering over the book, or rooted below it, was the obvious spirit of the writer and farmer Wendell Berry, whom
McKibben acknowledges by dedicating the book to him. I
think it's fair to say that Berry is one of the most influential
environmental thinkers of our time, and to anyone familiar
with the work of the Sage of Kentucky, the themes here
will ring familiar: the need to return to caring for our local
places; the need, in fact, to marry those places instead of
having strip-mining flings with them; the need to live—and
eat—from our proverbial backyard. It's the opposite of
globalization: it is *localization*, or at least regionalization.

Surprisingly, Berry's own literary godfather, Thoreau,
is not quoted once in McKibben's book. Maybe he's trying

to avoid the old-fashioned, romantic associations of one
of our most famous neck-bearded writers, but of course
everything McKibben argues for can be found right there in
Thoreau's *Walden*: commitment to the local, fighting against
the destruction of the natural world, and the big question,
why not be happy with less? By saying that McKibben owes
debts to Berry and Thoreau I am not trying to diminish his
book or argument. The book, I believe, is aimed at opening up more people to what until now has been the belief
of a few. It tries to make us face the fact that the SUV and
Trophy Home Party is almost over, and that morning in
America is actually going to be one doozy of a hangover.
Or to put it another way, it's time to face what we've put
off. To put up or shut up. Pay the bill. All that. In contrast
to Thoreau and Berry's more poetic means, McKibben's
argument for less is straightforward. But for all the straight-
forwardness, when I finished the book, I was left with a
simple question: will it work? Can a book like *Deep Economy*
ever truly galvanize its readers? Are we ready for the ideas
that Jimmy Carter tried to quietly sell us thirty years ago
before he and his cardigan sweater were run out of town?

I'm not sure. Clearly McKibben has his facts straight,
and his presentation of the Walmart-ization of America
is compelling. In our quest to be bigger and richer, always
bigger and richer, we have given the keys of the kingdom
to the very few and—surprise, surprise—those few don't
seem overly concerned with the common good. McOil and
McFood serve up the slop and we line up at the communal
troughs just like the cattle and chicken we're about to eat.
It's a gruesome picture built on greed. Sadly, I'm pretty sure
it's also an accurate picture. But I'm not sure if it's a picture
most of us are ready to see, or to think about a lot, let alone

fight against. And I'm not so sure about the way McKibben presents it either.

Here is what is wrong and here is what we need to do to fix it, he says very rationally. *Here is the virtuous course . . . here is what is* good. But doing what is virtuous has never been the world's greatest motivator. Our internal computers don't simply calculate what is right, and then act accordingly. Think again of those moments when Reagan came rushing in and swept Carter back off to the South. For the first (and maybe only) time a President mouthed ideas similar to Berry's and McKibben's: admitting doubt about our mania for growth, suggesting something as radical as a little restraint. And where did it get him? Carter's decline has become a cliché of our collective political memory: the dour little minister, shrinking every day in both political cartoons and the eyes of his countrymen, urging us to spend less on gas and turn down our thermostats. Our response? "How *dare* he?!"

If anything led to the orgy of consumption that followed it was the fear of being Carter as much as the love of all things Reagan. You think we should get *smaller*? Okay, then we'll build bigger cars and (much) bigger houses! You think we should lead a life, in Robert Frost's words, "of self-restraint for the common good"? Well, said most of my college friends, "Watch out Wall Street here I come!" We were so collectively frightened by the idea of restraint, of actually getting smaller, of running out of our great national abundance, that we, instead of meekly retiring, burst out into the world like a bunch of drunken frat boys, buying, eating, and drinking. The next Democratic President after Carter at least had the decency to be a big-eating, adultery-loving, excessive omnivore like the rest of us. No talk of "restraint" from Slick Willy. He didn't want to just grow the economy; he wanted it to burst out and swallow the rest of the world. It's the appetite, stupid.

So here comes McKibben, well-armed with knowledge but somewhat Carter-like in approach, telling us to get small. Will we listen? Are we finally ready? We now have a President who seems able to present Carter-like ideas with a shinier varnish, but the environment continues to register dead last on the list of people's actual concerns despite all the hollering about the end of the world.

Still, there are a few reasons for hope. McKibben has increasingly catalogued compelling stories—emphasis on *stories*—of people who have gone small and lived to tell the tale. And, suddenly, a lot more people seem to know what global warming is, and many also seem to know that the solution has something to do with paring back, not just inventing new Jetson-like gizmos to save our future. It's true that a single terrorist attack might knock environmental concerns off the front pages, but *for now*. . . .

For now a lot of people have embraced McKibben's fellow rationalist, Albert Gore, and for a while seemed honestly responsive when he pointed at his charts and graphs and, like your eccentric uncle, insisted on showing off his slideshow. But the response to him wasn't just to his rational argument, it was an emotional reaction; to the fact he lost an election he won and then grew a beard; to the fact he got depressed and then came back from the dead; suddenly he was living the life he wanted to live, fighting his own fight. It's like this: If we want a majority of people to actually act, if people are going to do the next-to-impossible, which is to say, *change their behavior*, there always needs to be emotional content, strong emotional connection

to the appeal. Maybe that's why, despite our tendency to
roll our eyes, it's not so awful to have Schwarzenegger
on the cover of magazines or to rent a polar bear for
photo ops or even to use the silly phrase "eco-warrior."
Gore himself seems to think that our tendency to have
visceral reactions is a bad thing—the result of too much
television—but it wasn't television that made England rally
around Churchill. Would the phrase *It is in our best interests
not to become extinct* have stirred people like Churchill's "I
have nothing to offer but blood, toil, tears, and sweat"?

And what does Dan Driscoll have in common with
Winston Churchill? What do little fights have to do with the
bigger struggle? Well, maybe fights like Dan's are relevant
because they incite on a personal level. We are Americans,
after all, and, for better or worse, we're well trained to fight,
to compete, for our personal and individual interests. Some
of the best fighters for the environment—Roosevelt, Muir,
Thoreau—have taken that same passionate individualism
and fought to save the land. Maybe it's too much to ask for
us to change our basic, excessive characters, but perhaps
we can turn that aggressive nature toward something else
and get competitive about, say, our car's mileage or saving yarn. Yes, what McKibben says is right—what Carter
said so long ago was right, or at least the beginning of
something right—but maybe the reason some are finally
starting to react is that it is being presented not as a true
fight to save the planet, but *as a fight to save our homes*. It's
easy to laugh at this, easy to picture the blockbuster with
Bruce Willis being called out of retirement to battle rising
sea levels or changing weather patterns, but silly or not, it
may be more *effective* for us to think this way. After all, who
among us can change our obsession with the individual that

much, or that fast? If we are individuals and fighters, so be it. But one thing we can do is turn that energy toward a good fight, and we don't need to look farther than our own home to find one. In this sense I hope the glossy magazines keep plastering those eco-celebrities and polar bears on their covers. Anything that helps. Anything that ignites.

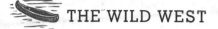 THE WILD WEST

We may paddle fast but that does not seem to translate into
boat speed. In one short day, I have managed to aid and abet
in destroying Dan's cherished canoe, the one he paddled
when he first explored and fought for the Charles. It is
canoe-icide, plain and simple. And yet Dan and I are feeling
guiltless. We keep laughing as we bail. It seems funny somehow to have almost destroyed our already limited adventure.

After awhile, the murky water inside the boat becomes
too deep and we pull over for repairs and food. We find a
beautiful sandbar in the middle of the current, and drag
the boat and ourselves out of the water. After dumping the
water, we eat a soggy lunch and drink a couple of beers.
The sandbar is a small hump in the middle of a copper-
colored section of river that is only a few canoe lengths
wide; the battered watercraft itself rests next to us, like
an injured friend, as we sip beers and stare at damselflies
skitting above the river. I watch the current part around
our little island. I feel adventurous, though I know the
rapids we ran were relatively tame as whitewater goes.

Dan feels it, too. It isn't easy spending your life banging
your head against a bureaucracy. It's important to get out
once in a while to see what you're fighting for.

Which is a long-winded way of saying we are in pretty
good moods while we eat lunch. This is why I do this shit.
To feel like this. To eat lunch that feels like necessary suste-
nance and not a habitual point in the day. To spend a whole

day outdoors. To feel tired and free — to have these hours
away from normal life.

For most of the morning the banks have been wooded,
but now, across from our sandbar, a wide lawn rolls up
to a gigantic new house. I worry that we are lunching on
private property, but Dan assures me that while the riverbank may belong to the homeowner, the little island we
are lunching on belongs to the state. Moreover, it is the
property of the citizens of the state, which means us.

He points to the way the lawn has been mowed right
down to the river's edge.

"We should get someone out here to sue their asses," he
says. He explains that the Wetlands Protection Act specifies
that you can't cut riparian wetlands and that a setback of
fifty to one hundred feet is required. I pull my tape recorder
out of my backpack and ask him if he'd like to put his opin-
ions on record.

"Yes, I'd be happy to," he says. "You can quote me as saying that these people, by cutting the bank and creating lawn
right to the edge, are definitely violating the law. And we
hate them for the vermin they are."

Then he points his beer at a statue of what appears to be
a fox or coyote.

"The owners put them there to scare the Canada geese
away, because they don't want the goose shit," he says. "Of
course they wouldn't have geese if they didn't mow their
lawn like that."

The main problem with the river, he explains, used to be
water quality, but much has changed since the Clean Water
Act. Now huge stripers chase herring eight miles upriver in
the once-famously dirty water.

"The problem now is quantity, not quality," he explains.

"The suburban towns siphon off the river so they can water their fucking lawns. It just makes so much more sense to let the native species grow. No need to water then. And it looks so much better."

To his eye, he doesn't add. He cracks open another beer and waxes eloquent for a while about the evils of mowing.

While he talks I think: If Dan is an admittedly limited, and hypocritical, environmentalist, then this wilderness he has spent the last two decades fighting for is certainly a limited wild. Before I moved back East I lived in Colorado for six years, and my Western friends would have a hard time imagining such a thing as a "wild Charles." Both their idea of what wilderness is, and their politics, are more ambitious and extreme. They want big wilderness, and I'm with them in spirit. I want big wilderness too. But Dan's, and really the majority of human's wilderness at this point is, of necessity, a limited wilderness.

Something about the morning's adventure—maybe the *yee-hah* aspect—reminds me of my years in Colorado. It seems everyone I knew there was always hiking and climbing up something or paddling and paragliding down. Though we are gliding through the most Eastern of wildernesses this morning, floating toward the snooty wilds of Harvard, my mind begins to migrate Westward. And I like it. "Go West, young brain!"

Dan lived in Colorado, too, and spent years camping in the West before heading back to fight for his first, Eastern wilderness. It occurs to me that one aspect of Dan's myth, and of my emerging picture of a new environmentalism, is the vital importance of the West, or at least something wild like the West. To paraphrase Gary Snyder: "The *West* is the place without fathers." One of the reasons that

the West is so important to the language and psychology
of environmentalism is that it is the one region that has
managed to tell a more romantically compelling story
about humans and nature. It is both a sexier, gun-slinging
narrative, and a more free-spirited, radical story. Eastern
environmentalism and global environmentalism could
learn a thing or two from Western environmentalism.
It's an environmentalism tinged with adventure, danger,
boldness—the land is bigger and so are the fights. While
environmentalism ultimately serves the conservation ethic
of Aldo Leopold, and is more about the whole than about
individuals, common sense suggests that it starts with
individuals; individuals spur change and so it is necessary
for those individuals to get excited and to take action.
In general, the West frames this appeal better than the
East: John Muir holding on to the top of a tree during a
lightning storm trumps Thoreau taking tea at Walden.

I try to explain this to Dan as we sit on our sandbar, but
my words trip over themselves. Still, he gets the gist of what
I'm saying, bringing up one of his heroes, Bob Marshall,
who, he tells me, managed to roam large swaths of the
West and found the Wilderness Society before dying young
at thirty-eight.

"He was a model for me," Dan says. "Not the dying
part, but the activism tied to actually getting out there.
Getting outside. I try to do what he did. I mean, the
Charles is not the Colorado. But he was still a model."

I mention my fondness for Ed Abbey. Abbey's books, like
Desert Solitaire and *The Monkey Wrench Gang*, had meant a lot
to me, in no small part because they suggested a different
way of being "environmental." While most environmental
writing has overly proper manners, Abbey revived the old

Western tradition of braggadocio and boastfulness, waxing poetic about a twisting desert juniper in one sentence
and unleashing an anti-immigration tirade in the next that
left your jaw dropping. On the one hand he wrote paeans
to solitude; on the other, he told fart jokes. Though often
poetic and high-minded, he seemed to embrace his own
id; he was passionately lecherous, a desert Henry Miller.
He kept his readers off guard, and until you figured him
out, if you ever did, surprise was on his side: What would
this hairy, bearded, cigar-smoking booze-swilling barbarian
do next?

I try to explain to Dan how my own ethic changed during my years living in the West.

"It became bigger, feistier," I say.

"That's right," he says. "We need more fight out here.
We need to take something from the West. We need bigger
stories."

Dan is right. He—we—are on to something. Perhaps
one of the most important contributions of Western
environmentalism is to break us out of Walden and add an
element of senselessness and outrageousness and humor
to the fight. To add both a sense of individualism and its
opposite, the sense of belonging to a small group fighting the bigwigs. And of course: to do all this, as Dan says,
while *outside*. Maybe this is too romantic, but romanticism
has its uses, and one of those uses is to excite people.

Dan tells me about a couple of his hiking trips out West,
and then I tell him about a recent trip to Moab, Utah, to
meet one of Ed Abbey's oldest friends, a riverman who
shared spirit, if not geography, with Dan. The drive west
from Grand Junction, dropping down from Colorado into
Utah is, for my money, the most beautiful in the world. Dan

was obviously exaggerating earlier when he suggested that
we should all take mushrooms, but if you want to get a
taste of the experience without the fungi, I suggest the drive
along the river into Moab, which provides a fairly reasonable
simulation.

You descend into a strange red dream world of hoo-
doos and mesas and buttes, a world of twisted sandstone
of such mystic power that that even multiple SUV com-
mercials can't desecrate it. As you drop off the highway
and head south along Route 128, driving through canyons
parallel to the twisting Colorado River, with barely another car in sight, it's hard to build up too much ire about
how tourists are overrunning the West. It becomes less
hard forty miles later when you pass the spanking-new
Sorrel River Ranch development, a theme park cluster
of buildings that inhabit a place where I used to unroll
my sleeping bag on a sandbar not too many years back.
And it gets plain easy when you enter Moab itself.

It's a town every bit as biblical as its name. Here is
where the battle between the new and old West truly
rages. Moab has ridden the highs and lows of both ura-
nium mining and mountain biking, and if you wanted to
stage a gunfight between an old timer and a fannypack-
wearing bicyclist you could find no better setting than
Main Street. Though, on second thought, there would
barely be room for it. RVs rumble down the streets and
a hundred gaudy signs try to draw in the tourists, like
beckoning recreational prostitutes, selling, instead of sex,
rafting and biking and jeep tours. Think Vegas for out-
doorsmen. Beamed down onto Main Street, an extra-
terrestrial could be forgiven for concluding that the word
ADVENTURE was the most common one on our world.

Up above Moab, amid blazing yellow aspens in the La
Sal Mountains, you can look down at multiple red-rock
towers like a series of giant, misplaced chess pieces. There
you will find the Pack Creek Ranch and there I found Ken
Sleight, the eighty-year-old former river rafter and horse-
man who was the inspiration for Seldom Seen Smith, the
wildly adventurous "Jack Mormon" who appeared in Ed
Abbey's best-known novel, *The Monkey Wrench Gang*. I
rented a cabin in Pack Creek for two nights, and discovered
Sleight over by his truck the next morning. He was wearing jeans and two dungaree shirts, despite the early heat.
I told him I was heading into town to get a cup of coffee — I certainly did not tell him that the coffee would be
a soy latte, light on the foam — and asked if we could meet
up later. He said sure and pointed to where he'd be — "My
office" — an aluminum-roofed bunker above his horse
pasture. Later, caffeinated, I sat across from him while he
stretched his legs out and regaled me with stories of his
early days as one of Utah's original river guides. We had
only talked for twenty minutes when he asked me if I
wanted a beer. So I chased my latte with a Milwaukee's Best
while he told stories of floating down the river with Abbey.

"We both loved it all — the goofing off, the food,
being part of the crew. Lots of good happens on those
trips — they're so spontaneous and joyful. It's true: most
campfires are very joyous. Very romantic. There's a sense
that everything is right in the realm."

At one point I sheepishly confessed that I'd been a
mountain biker, and asked him what he, having spent most
of his life living near Moab, made of the biking craze.

"Well, I don't think they hurt the land all that much.
Mostly what they hurt is the spirit of the wilderness.

I'll be out taking a hike and they'll come roaring down. Never one of them, of course. They run in packs in those colorful clothes. Anytime you bring fashion into wilderness I think you're in trouble. I think I'd like to get on my horse and ride down into town all clad in Spandex. Just to show them how ridiculous they look."

I laughed, picturing Sleight, grizzled with white hair and shining blue eyes below his shaggy white-gray eyebrows, decked out in skin-tight clothes.

"I'd do it too," he said "I'd put the tight Spandex over my asshole body and get on my horse and boy, would I shine. It would just be a symbol of course, but there's value in a symbol."

He took a sip of his beer and leaned back.

"I have no problem making an ass of myself," he said.

Which, I've come to believe, is a valuable tool. Ken Sleight, like his old friend Ed Abbey, still knew a thing or two about the importance of grand symbolic gestures, gestures that can sometimes make you look silly. When Sleight ran for the State Legislature a decade ago, registering hundreds of previously unregistered Native Americans in the process, he vowed to ride up the State House steps on his horse if he won.

Around that time he made a similar gesture when he discovered that loggers were deforesting the nearby Amasa Back wilderness, dragging chained trees over Native American archeological sites. What further outraged Sleight was the fact that the logging was going on without the required BLM (Bureau of Land Management) monitor. So he climbed on his horse and rode up the mountainside to confront the loggers.

"I pulled up in front of them so that they had to either

stop or run me over," he told me that morning in his trailer. "My horse bucked when they kept coming. But they finally stopped. We had a standoff until the cops came. I was hoping they would arrest me but they didn't. You can say it was just a symbol but the next time they logged they had a BLM man with them."

When I think about the state of the environmental movement today, this is what I think: Not only do we need more guys who stop the bad guy loggers on horseback but we need more *stories* about men and women who stop the bad guy loggers on horseback. That is, we need more eco-legends or, as the writer Jack Turner would have it, we need *lore*.

An obvious reason that the American West plays such a vital role in our current environmental thinking is that, as Dan said, the fights are starker there, the land bigger. There's more to lose. The memory of the wild past is less distant. But lore may be another reason that the West is so important; not just its realities but also its language. I think of Terry Tempest Williams singing ecstatic praises of her red rock desert, but also working to pass the Escalante wilderness bill through Congress. I think of Dave Foreman who, influenced in part by Ed Abbey literary monkeywrenching, went on to found Earth First! And I think of Susan Zakin, an environmental journalist and novelist who would chronicle Dave Foreman's exploits in her first book, *Coyotes and Town Dogs*. In that book Zakin, calling Foreman and his gang "buckaroos," describes the origin story of Earth First! as a fateful trip away from civilization to the Pinacate Desert in 1980 during which the group decided that *they* would break from the more stodgy style of environmentalism that had prevailed in organizations like the Sierra

Club. In other words, they decided to take matters into
their own hands: advocating monkey-wrenching, disabling
bulldozers, and cutting down billboards and spiking trees.

And of course, inevitably, they indulged in that greatest of Western eco-obsessions: battling against the building
of dams. Dams, from Hetch Hetchy to Dinosaur Canyon
to Glen Canyon, are central to the eco-myths of the West.
John Muir set the tone when he famously employed biblical language to rail against the developers who would
build a dam that would flood his beloved Hetch Hetchy
Valley: "These temple destroyers, devotees of ravag-
ing commercialism, seem to have a perfect contempt for
Nature, and, instead of lifting their eyes to the God of the
mountains, lift them to the Almighty Dollar." Ed Abbey
kept the invective up when he railed against the flooding
of Glen Canyon, calling it the "damnation of a canyon."

For Ken Sleight the death of Glen Canyon and the creation of Lake ~~Meade~~ Powell by the Glen Canyon Dam was almost
unbearable.

"I'd been thinking about it for a long time before it
happened," Sleight said to me. "I loved those side canyons and those arches and couldn't imagine them buried
in a big bathtub. The total realization of the enormity of
it all didn't hit me until they started building the dam. It
was physically painful. I felt rage. And deep sadness."

Fittingly, the Glen Canyon Dam was Earth First!'s first
strike. This act was a symbolic one, when, with Abbey
himself in attendance, they unfurled a giant three hundred
foot sheet with an illustration of a crack on it in front of the
dam, making it appear the dam itself was splitting. It was, as
I say, a symbolic event, with no policy repercussions, and in
truth a large part of Earth First!'s importance over the next

decade was symbolic. But that is not to say it wasn't effective. Symbols, like the image of Ken Sleight stopping the
loggers on horseback, play an import role in environmental
fights and what Earth First! symbolized was a new kind of
environmentalism, something more dangerous, and more
fun, than old school environmentalism. Of course Earth
First! would soon enough be tarred with the brush of ter-
rorism, and the FBI would crack down and the party would
be over. But before the party ended the organization opened
a window into which some could peek and maybe get an
idea of what a future environmental movement might look
like. That movement would be kind of wild, kind of fun,
and would have a communal sense of a band of fighters, of
merry men and women, fighting against the powers that be.
Thumbing their nose, giving the collective finger, all that.

I am aware that these buckaroos and nose-thumbers
only make up one front in the overall environmental war.
The Nordhauses and Shellenbergers make up another, a
very necessary front, pushing policy through and working
in the bureaucratic mines. Furthermore, there are plenty of
big problems with the Ed Abbey mythology, even beyond
the obvious one that his macho rants take occasional de-
tours into the sexist and xenophobic. As much as I may like
the idea of the environmental fighter as a Rooster Cogburn
character, taking the reins in his mouth and his six-guns in
hand, after yelling out to the enemy, "Fill yer hand you son
of a bitch," I must admit that the cowboy myth has some
serious limitations.

Which is not to say it should be tossed out altogether. It
just needs some revision. Ken Sleight himself seemed surprisingly receptive to this idea, surprisingly ready to acknowledge his own hypocrisy and contradictions. Ken had grown

up in a conservative Western home, but had, in his words, "evolved."

He, too, worried about a distortion and oversimplification of the standard Western myths. He admitted that despite his own bursts of civil disobedience, and the fact that some people thought he was "way out there," he had actually spent the better part of his life in the tourism business running his rafting company and felt some culpability in Moab's recreation boom.

"When I went down the river with Abbey we were both kind of like double agents. We both loved the wildness of it all, but at the same time we had our *uses* for the thing. He was always writing and thinking about the places and people we were with. He was doing it with his writing and I was doing it with the trips. 'Come with me and I'll show you Cathedral in the Desert.'

"I remember when I was living down in Escalante, taking trips down Escalante Canyon to Coyote Gulch. When I first went there the place was empty and I would put out these little mimeographed sheets in town, trying to drum up business. But then I took some reporters from *Sunset* magazine down the river and they wrote an article on me. A few weeks later I saw people hiking in the canyon and when I asked them they said yes, they had read the article. And people led to more people. I began to see you had to be careful. Began to see you could love a place to death."

His motivation for taking the reporters along had been a simple economic one — "Heck, I could do a little better" — and Sleight admitted he had had his hand in how things ended up going. What he was admitting to, in effect, was being one of Dan Driscoll's hypocrites. But he had also tried to slow things down, fighting to regulate and keep roads out of Moab. In fact, many of Sleight's battles over the last four decades had been, despite his cowboy image, efforts at restraint.

Perhaps this is where the revision of the cowboy myth begins. For years now the free market de-regulators, with Ronald Reagan as their hero, have claimed the cowboy as their own. But there are other uses of that myth. Think of those who have gone wild in the West, then turned around—wildly, romantically—and spread the word that the West was a place for inspiration, though also a place that could not hold too many people.

"Lawlessness, like wildness, is attractive, and we conceive the last remaining home of both to be in the West," wrote Wallace Stegner.[10] Yes, we come West for that feeling of wildness, of lawlessness too, the sense that we can do what we want and on our own. But in these days of crushing numbers, one person's freedom impacts the freedom of a hundred others.

Even though the idea of a conservationist cowboy may be confusing, it's also useful. If we are looking for stories that spark, this is a good place to start. When I lived in the West, I watched with my own eyes as formerly un-environmental friends read Abbey and changed. So I know it can happen. Absorbing the romance of Abbey's wildness doesn't mean you need to be yet one more Patagonia-clad emigrant in one of a million over-populated, under-watered cities. It is a question of spirit, not style.

After leaving, Ken I also spoke with Kristin McKinnon, a modern day Ken Sleight and the owner of Wild Rivers Expeditions. "The river corridors are being used like never before," she said. "But with care and effort you can take people to still-wild places. There's still a lot here. The important thing is to make our impact minimal. I like to think that people will return home more inclined to protect the places they live in. Spending time outside in a beautiful place will trigger this."

In the end, the cowboy myth is just a kick-start, something that, with any luck, will get us thinking. We may love the wild myths but the larger reality is that it will require some restraint if we are to preserve these final wild patches. There is no reason the cowboy myth of Bush and Reagan can't turn back into the cowboy myth of Teddy Roosevelt. Maybe the work ahead, as Ken Sleight has discovered, is the work of reigning in as much as letting—*yee-haw*—loose. And maybe, paradoxically, restraint—an uncharacteristic but evolved restraint—is the road to preserving what freedom is left in the not-so-wild West.

If it is true that the greater Western fight is sometimes more complicated than I have made it out to be, that policy and regulation and restraint are a large part of that fight, it is also true that we can still take from those old, complicated Western myths a dash of romance. In short, I don't want to throw the cowboy out with the bath water. For the moment I want to keep my focus on the more romantic stories—keep the focus on Ken Sleight sitting on his horse in front of the loggers—and I do this for a practical reason. I am interested in what makes someone, particularly a young someone, begin to fight for the environment. If we are looking for stories that ignite, that engage, there is no better place. The West still offers us a greater sense of adventure, of outrageousness, of *fun*. And daring. All these qualities will come in handy in making the environmental vocation not just something more rounded, but something that people may actually want to do.

THE IRISH ALEHOUSE

Dan, as he admits, has borrowed freely from Western myths, and has brought many things back East with him. But his sense of fun, of wildness and humor, is balanced by a sort of stolid common sense. He isn't Ed Abbey sawing down billboards or walking for days alone in the canyons. And he knows he isn't about to create a great trackless wilderness in the Boston suburbs. As it was, the legislature scoffed at his early attempts to create a nature preserve along the Charles. Here common sense kicked in. To get his limited urban wildness, his practical political choice was to push for the creation of bike paths.

"Bike paths, you can get funding for," he explains as we lounge on the sandbar. "They don't give a shit about 'wilderness.' But bike paths they kind of understand. So you try to use federal money creatively by calling things 'bikeways' but you're really trying to establish a connection with nature. They don't review the grants that closely. I'll sneak in a hundred thousand dollars for native plantings and they will say okay."

As someone who commuted daily to work by bike, Dan knew the practical value of these paths. I remember the two years that I lived car-lessly and commuted in and out of work in Colorado, and I know that I lived differently during that time. Groceries became provisions and I thought hard about what I could carry, how much energy I would put out and take in.

For Dan, the paths were just a means to an end. It was through the funding for the paths that he would get what he really wanted. It didn't sound as romantic as "nature trails" but no one was about to give him money for those. Bike paths became his Trojan horse. They allowed him to re-plant the banks and return some wildness to the river.

✕

It would be nice to simply sleep here on our sandbar. Right in the rich guy's backyard, with nothing he could do about it. But we have places to be, and so, finally, reluctantly, we stand up and push off. The mansions of Wellesley and Dover are behind us, and, as we enter Needham and Dedham, the river takes a decidedly urban turn. We are in a kind of transition zone where the household incomes will be half of what they were where we started. If the Charles has a St. Louis Arch of sorts, letting you know you have entered new territory, it is Route 128. We cross quietly, unseen, under the unending roar of the highway's six lanes, moving through the gateway to the city river.

The sight of it sets Dan off on another tirade.

"Each of these bridges costs millions to maintain and it's where most of our public money is going. Right now we are spending over a hundred million on the Longfellow Bridge. Maybe there are enough bridges into the city already. What if we just didn't fix it? What if we made it into a walking bridge? There are enough roads in the city already."

He is quiet for a minute but clearly not done.

"Give me a third of what it takes to fix one bridge and I'll make a complete circuit of paths of all of Boston's rivers." He is excited now and he could go on . . . of course he could . . . but soon, the urban landscape rising around us distracts him.

"The strange thing is that folks in the suburbs place great value on this land along the river," Dan says. "But once you get here, in the city itself, it is devalued."

The places we pass prove his point: industrial parks, car lots, chain link fences right on the river. After its stately ramble through the large-lawned suburbs, the Charles turns gritty.

"Of course the land should be *more* valuable here, where it's the only contact point with nature," he adds. But for one reason or another, it's not. Dan plans to change that. He has vowed to revitalize this area as well. He points out that even here people are already trying to connect to the river: a hole in the fence yawns and some- one has plopped an old, stuffed chair above the riverbank where they can creep down during their lunch break to watch the river flow; workers sneaking out the factory's back door for lunch or a cigarette or maybe, on Fridays, a beer; looking down at the river and seeing where it had come from and where it was flowing; a place to briefly escape their jobs, sure, but also a point of contact.

True, it isn't the nature you find in *Sierra* magazine. It is not distant, pristine, and pure. It is not the nature of the na- tional park, the nature you need to drive or fly to see. Instead it's the nature of the creek that runs through your neighbor- hood, the nature of the abandoned lot, the nature of the small secret patch of beach protected by rocks. I understand that there are those who would scoff at my trying to make claims of wilderness for Needham. But I think we are making a deadly mistake if we ignore the smaller, more compromised patches, since that is what so many of us are left with.

$\times$

Even though my feelings about wildness and wilderness
are instinctive, my ideas about wildness have evolved. Back
in the spring of 2001, I began paying visits to an old man
named John Hay. At the time I was still living on Cape Cod,
just down the street from Hay, but this man, regarded by
many as our greatest living nature writer, was no ordinary
neighbor. He was eighty-six, and still had the energy to hike
through the trees and walk the beaches around his home on
Dry Hill in Brewster, where he had lived for sixty years. He
liked to pluck a leaf or flower and jam it under my nose and
order me to smell it before identifying it for me. Though
I'd been writing about the natural world myself for over
ten years, it would not be going too far to say that my visits
with John began to deepen, if not change, the way I thought
about nature.

John deeply believes that there isn't one box called
NATURE and another box called HUMAN BEINGS. "Many
people write about saving the environment," he said in
a 1978 speech to the Cape Cod Museum of History. "But
you can't save a thing unless you feel you are a part of it."
Even in this increasingly fragmented and specialized age
of cell phones and online gratification, this is true. But to
understand this, to really believe it and feel it and live it, is a
hard task.

Wendell Berry once wrote that his greatest ambition was
to belong to the place he lived, the way the local muskrats might. To many of us, this might seem to be going a
little far, but I like the way the word "ambition" is lodged
in the middle of his statement. If we environmentalists
try to re-make humans as ambition-less, floating Zen-like
creatures, we are doomed. Humans are always driven
and prodded by goals, by curiosity, by pushing forward

to new places. But as Berry says of his own ambition to belong to a place, ". . . I have come to see that it proposes an enormous labor. It is a spiritual ambition, like good-ness."[11] In other words it isn't easy to belong to a place, to accept that we are part of a larger animal world, but the fact that it isn't easy doesn't make it any less vital to *try*. As it turns out gaining humility is not always a humble enterprise. Berry, for instance, has spent a lifetime stum-bling toward his goal. He's never fully succeeded, but in his trying he's found new depths of living well in the world.

My own goal is slightly different than Berry's and Hay's. Unlike them, I have not spent a lifetime committing to one place. For instance, I left Cape Cod five years ago and now live in coastal North Carolina, where I teach at a univer-sity, so I can't very well claim that I will "marry" my home place. But what I can claim is this: I will work to keep my life wild. Not frat boy wild, mind you, even if there is the occasional beer, or four, consumed. But wild as in spontane-ous, creative, and open. Wild as in spending a part of each day on the beach or in the woods or in the mountains.

Wild as in joyful. Which may be why I so object to an environmentalism that focuses on the merely tragic — the photos-of-clubbing-baby-seals approach. When we talk about nature it doesn't have to sound like socialist propaganda. It's strange really, that so much writing about the natural world should leave us feel-ing so dour when, for the most part, the overwhelming experience of wildness is *fun*. This is the part that people forget when they get all do-gooder-y about the environ-ment. Thoreau the environmentalist was just Thoreau the man after all. And though he was many things, I like him best when he was the man who said this: "I would

like to say a word in favor of wildness." Wildness. Not
really the kind of value you find on many political agendas, but one you do still find on human agendas.

I am not taking anything away from environmentalists or environmental policy. I'm just saying that there's a
deeper story here, a deeper level below the merely "environmental," I'm saying that this deeper story is the one that
those who we consider the fountainheads of environmental
thought — Muir, Thoreau, Leopold, and Carson — learned
and then brought back to the world. These stories begin not
with ideas but with joy. With a kind of primitive delight in
the world. With the mad fact of the world — aspen leaves
fluttering, copper creeks flowing, waves crashing again
and again forever, sunsets dipping down nightly, gaudy and
overdone. And the deeper story begins not with theory
but with particular places — a cove in Maine, a canyon in
California, a pond in Massachusetts — particular places
that particular *Homo sapiens* fall deeply and strangely in
love with. Later all this becomes laws and rules and books
and essays. But it begins well before and well below that.
What later becomes words begins with wordlessness.

Which is why I continue to stress the word *wild* in
these decidedly un-wild times. I stress it because it is vital,
because without it all is lost. It is the wellspring, the unnamed, the ineffable, the slightly crazy, the fickle, the
joyous, the strange, and the creative force behind so much
of what we feel and do. I stress it because, no matter how
we plan or make things-to-do lists, and no matter how we
try, valiantly and importantly, to control events, every great
act depends on something beyond our control, something
unpredictable and wordless. In short, something wild.

If we don't acknowledge this, if we don't believe this,

then there is no real reason to stop stamping out the wild. There is no reason not to continue to make our world as predictable, efficient, virtual, and calculated as possible. And there's no argument against the logic of the assembly line or the music of automation. If we don't believe this then taking any action to protect the wild is just another logical decision: Why, yes, I think it makes good sense to save the rainforest just in case there are unknown plants there that could provide medicines to cure human illnesses.

Screw that. Of course there isn't anything wrong with finding medicines, curing illnesses, recycling aluminum cans, twisting in light bulbs, attending meetings, putting a stop to the local cement plant, and printing on both sides of the paper. In fact there's a whole lot right about these things, and they are necessary in this time of crisis. All I am really saying is that there is something else that is important as well, something deeper, something not just right but joyous.

When we set out this morning, Dan thought the land next to Long Ditch would be a good spot for the night's camping. Long Ditch is an artificial tributary of the Charles which was excavated by citizens of Dedham in 1654 in an effort to reduce flooding of the town's lowlands.[12] As we approach, the ditch looks, to my eye, very ditch-like: The mucky banks lead up to chest high grasses, which I imagine are filled with ticks.

I suggest we camp in the woods nearby.

"The woods aren't safe once you get this close to the city. We're better off on state land—no one comes here." He explains that the land is owned by the DCR, the Department of Conservation and Recreation, the organization that he works for, and is separated from the parklands by the moat of the ditch itself. Then he adds: "This grass is too high for ticks." I'm not so sure about that but we tie up our boat to the root of a willow tree and then Dan charges into the grasses using his oar as a machete to hack clear a place for our tent.

We set up camp and celebrate with beers in the matted-down front yard of our temporary home. The beer works its everyday magic. We lie back on the grass despite my worries about ticks and an odd rustling sound nearby in the higher grasses.

Dusk is approaching and, with our camp set up, we climb down the muddy bank to our boat. Our first job is bailing and we scoop out the stinking water. Then we climb back into the stinking boat in our stinking clothes and we paddle out of the ditch and onto Cow Island Pond. We work our way east across the pond, into the wind, toward the far end where the river intersects with Route One. The work is somewhat grueling, after a long day already, but the destination is a noble one: The Olde Irish Alehouse, a rickety wooden building. As we approach, it looms above us like a decrepit barge, seemingly ready to tumble into the river. The building is a kind of kitschy monument, dotted with leprechaun trinkets and crowned by a wooden sculpture of two swans that appear to be making out, but at least it, unlike so many of the nearby buildings, has not entirely turned its back on the river. The people dining two floors above us look down through the window and wave. We tie up to a tree root and scramble up a dirt bank near a dumpster and into the parking lot, observing multiple signs of civilization, including several gas stations, a Dunkin' Donuts, and an "Entering Boston" sign. We enter the building in our mucky clothes, but no one knows we have come by water. Inside we devour mashed potatoes and dangerously undercooked steaks and top it off with vodka gimlets.

✕

I like traveling with Dan. He is a good guide and a lot of fun, but there's something else that puts him above other co-pilots. He provides a relief, maybe even an antidote, to the tone of environmentalism that makes me want to thumb my nose and turn away. What continues to bug me, when it comes right down to it, is the sheer earnestness of environmentalism, the conviction that the world is doomed and the compulsive need to share this cheery news. If there were environmental weather reports, they would go something like this: "Gloom expected today . . . more doom tomorrow."

Of course the world is doomed. Human beings cover the earth like maggots, species are wiped out daily, land is gobbled up by developers, the great migrations are dying out, the world is warming, sea level rising. All true. And then throw in the fact that while all this is going on most people seem less concerned with the fate of the world than with the fate of the latest starlet to enter rehab. Nature writers are accused of being apocalyptic, but the facts themselves are pretty dire.

Which tends to have this result: Human beings, most of whom are not really very good at dwelling in hopelessness, turn away. Maybe it's just too much for the human mind to live in a constant state of world anxiety. It not only doesn't help the mind much; it only rarely helps the world. Yes, there are some great, galvanizing, world-saving personalities—we live in desperate times and it's true

that desperation can sometimes energize. But hopelessness, as a rule, does *not* inspire. We are not very good at
fighting apocalypses. We are better at fighting for our
neighborhoods or for sections of river we've grown up on.
And most of us need at least a dollop of hope to nudge
ourselves into action. Again, I'm not talking about Disney
hope here but a practical hope, hope in the face of reality.

It does seem hopeful to me that, paddling into a city
of over four million, we can still see a deer on the banks,
a sharp-shinned hawk in the canopy, stripers swimming
below. And it does seem hopeful that imperfect human
beings, crazy eyed, former deadheads like Dan, have
fought to correct our mistakes and redeem something that
seemed unredeemable, like this river. It's not the ultimate
answer, but it's something. The beginning of something.
Something to create momentum, to fight inertia.

Whenever I think of small fights, I think of the writer
Joy Williams, and what she did with her home in Key West.
She bought a house there decades ago but before long a
suburb sprung up around her: manicured lawns, sprin-
klers, the works—all very "civilized." Joy, however, let her
plot of land grow wild, as it always had, with vines and
trees and lizards and snakes and ferns. When the neighbors started to complain she simply built a fence around
it, making her last stand there, letting her tiny ecosystem
thrive. When Joy and I first met she was staying at a beach
house on an overdeveloped coastal town in North Carolina
near where I teach, and sitting on the front porch of that
house, I noted that there was a single undeveloped plot
across the street where green herons had clustered at
dusk. It might have been the very last undeveloped plot
on the whole island, the last bit that wasn't concrete, and I

started to make a point of studying it, noticing that migrating birds seemed to know just where it was; this was
their stopover point. It occurred to me that while we need
people to fight for millions of acres in Utah, we also need
people to fight to save that single plot, that tiny wilderness.

I know that while a glimpse of a leaf through the bars
of a jailhouse may be a form of wilderness, it is not one
that would satisfy many of us. But I also find it hopeful that
even in this wounded landscape there are still delights to
being alive.

After more gimlets and dangerously raw meat, we finally
pay the bill and say goodbye to the Alehouse. Sliding down
the muddy bank, slightly unsteady, we clamber back into
the canoe and paddle home drunk to our murky campsite lit
with fireflies in the ditch. More lights come next. We stare
off toward town, where someone has decided to set off a
fairly impressive display of fireworks one day early. "A warm
up," Dan calls it.

We sleep well despite a strange rustling from some
creature in the tall grass that brings the movie *Alien* to mind.
I wake early and discover that someone has left a huge hob-
nailed boot on our campsite doorstep, footwear that looks
part angler's wader and part hooker boot. I am not sure
when or how it got here, but I know it was not here when
we arrived. We have truly entered the urban wild.

This is my wildness. A trashy ditch with a hooker boot for
flora. Maybe that's a good thing. Sometimes I don't think
people value wildness because they believe they have to

hike to the top of a mountain in Alaska to find it. I have
traveled all over the world to experience the wild, but
some of my wildest moments have been closer to home.
On Cape Cod, on the same domestic beach I've returned
to all my life—where the summer is all kids, umbrellas,
and beach balls—the winter cold clears it of people and its
character changes. From the rocks at the end of the beach
I once watched hundreds of snow-white gannets dive from
a hundred feet in the air, plunging into the freezing winter
ocean like living javelins. Then, as the birds dove down,
something else dove up: a breaching humpback whale rising as it herded the same fish the gannets were diving for.

"In wildness is the preservation of the world," wrote .
Thoreau, but as many others have pointed out, people
often get the quote wrong and use "wilderness" instead.[13]
While *wilderness* might be untrammeled land along the
Alaskan coast, *wildness* can happen anywhere. Wildness is
unplanned, unpredictable. You can't put a fence around it. It
can happen in the jungle or on a city river. It rises up when
you least expect it.

It is of vital importance that we not define this wildness as wilderness, that we not construct intellectual walls
between the natural and the human. In fact, it was while
observing my own species, my own family, that I experienced the two wildest moments of my life.

The first came while holding my father's hand while he
died. I listened to his final breaths, first deep and then gasp-
ing and fish-like, and I gripped his hand tight enough to feel
the last pulsings of his heart. Something rose in me that day,
something deep, animal, unexpected, something that I didn't
experience again until my daughter Hadley was born nine
years later. Before her birth everyone warned me that my

life was about to change, the implication being that it would become tamer. But there was nothing tame about those twenty-four hours in the hospital, or that indelible moment, after the C-section, when the doctor reached into my wife, up to his elbows, and a bloody head emerged, straight up, followed by Hadley's full emergence and a wild squall of life as her little arms rose over her head in victory. Sure the surge was physiological—goosebumps and tingling scalp and a hundred other physical symptoms—but it was more than that, too, a wild rush, both a loss of and a return to self.

These moments of death and life, as much as any moments in pristine nature, reconnect us to our primal selves, remind us that there is something wilder lurking below the everyday, that, having tasted wildness, we return to our ordinary lives both changed and charged. So while I will continue to seek out and protect wild places, I do so knowing that I don't need to travel to the Amazon or Everest to experience the ineffable. It is on that same Cape Cod beach where I first walked holding my mother's hand, near the waters where I later spread my father's ashes, that I learned that my wildest moments are often closest to home. And it is there that I now bring Hadley each summer, secretly hoping that the wild will rise up in her when she least expects it.

III. TRANSFORMATION

THE VISION THING

Dan snores in the tent while I read, taking breaks to listen to the orchard oriole that sings in the willow tree above our tent, offering a sweet accompaniment to Dan's glottal savagery. For most of the night I had been frightened for my life, but the rustling alien creature is apparently nocturnal— the grasses are now quiet. I wonder if it could have been a fisher. Whatever the case, it is a relief to no longer be stalked.

In fact it is a beautiful morning and if not for my lack of caffeine, and the book in my hands, I might feel quite peaceful. I look up again from *Break Through*, contemplating whether drowning or fire would be a better fate for these pages. It is sad that we have become so specialized that someone who writes about nature can feel so distant from someone responsible for writing the laws to save nature. We are separate tributaries off of the main Thoreauvian river, and we have branched off long ago and in separate directions.

I remember something Dan said to me last night, while we sipped our vodka and ate our steaks.

"I think of myself as a common, modern-day visionary," he said. "Understand that the emphasis is on *common*. The only reason I seem extraordinary is that in a business like mine, in any kind of government business, there are so few of us. In general the visionaries are cut out of the process. Instead you get little visionary blips like what I've done out here. But to make it happen I've had to leverage federal funds and get corporate help and convince people to give me their land.

"I've found that what Carnegie said is true. There is more money than there are good ideas. Get a good idea and the money follows.

"Of course, even when I pull in outside money I get crap for it. Here is what one of the administrators actually said: 'I'm tired of Dan Driscoll trying to leverage outside money to control what the state is going to do.' So if I said to him, 'I just got a four million dollar grant for us — and four-hundred thousand dollars of our funds will go to restoring this corridor.' But he feels like I'm forcing him to spend four-hundred thousand on something he didn't want to spend it on. And I'm saying, 'you don't want to spend it on anything good because you don't know anything good.' You're a bean counter. You shouldn't be involved in policy decisions. And people sit in rooms and people make decisions about how to spend billions of dollars. And they have no plan, no vision."

It was me, the choir, he was preaching to, but this morning his words also bear down on the book I'm reading. I can't help noticing the antipathy that Nordhaus and Shellenberger feel toward visionaries, and toward artists in particular. While they really don't seem to like nature and environmentalists that much, it's nothing compared to what they have to say about us poor writers. They'll quote Thoreau — who won't? — because he's safely dead and canonized. But the rest of us had better watch out. Most writers focusing on nature, according to the authors, go around claiming that nature is "above mankind." Artists believe, according to Nordhaus and Shellenberger, that anyone jimmying around with nature represents a kind of biblical fall (apparently they think our tribe doesn't use flush toilets or electric screwdrivers). They also politely lecture us, telling us—lo and behold, trumpets here please—that human beings are actually a part of nature too. What they might find if they picked up a book or two is that those who write and think about nature do so in a myriad of ways, just as people think about policy in different ways. They might find that there are ideas, outside of affluence and abundance, that move human beings.

Disdain might be too strong a word for how the authors feel about artists, but it's pretty close. I remember reading an interview in the online environmental magazine *Grist* with these two where they were asked why they'd exhaustively interviewed leading activists but not a single visionary thinker or writer—someone, for instance, like Wendell Berry. Nordhaus replied, "We interviewed the people in the environmental movement who are deciding how to spend tens of millions of dollars annually. . . . I'm sorry, Wendell Berry isn't the person deciding how the enviro movement is going to construct its campaigns to address global warming."[14]

And there it is. When it comes to their number one priority, forming a vision of a new environmentalism, Wendell Berry is not relevant. Wendell Berry, who has spent the last forty years or so fashioning an original, idiosyncratic, and brilliant body of work that often focuses on committing to, and fighting for, the places where we live. Nordhaus and Shellenberger argue against the false separation and specialization of different groups, but they apparently think they have nothing to learn from a mere writer. Which is more than a little problem. After all, if you are going to construct your argument around the need for a "vision," can you

really ignore visionaries? Can't they acknowledge that inspired words and inspired politics often go hand in hand? Art
isn't a box you can pack in the attic, far away from another
box called politics. Clearly a compelling vision, one that calls
us back to the natural world, is required before we get down
to the business of saving it.

I like arguing with Nordhaus and Shellenberger so
much that it's hard to stop but I finally put the book down.
The truth is that, for all my antipathy, we have more in
common than I'm admitting. They too want to create an
environmentalism that goes beyond the name, one that is
included in a larger politics. They are at their best when they
apply the principles of ecology to the wider political landscape, when they connect the economy to national security
to energy independence. This is the landscape they know
well, the ecotone of pragmatism and passion, and like naturalists they make connections within that ecosystem. Their
point is a good one. You can't look at "the environment"
alone; you need to see it, as any good ecologist will tell you,
in its greater ecosystems. I admire this. My only complaint
with their politics of inclusion is that they have excluded
two important elements: the storytellers, and nature.

I should add that Nordhaus and Shellenberger are not
entirely anti-artistic. They are fond of one form of art: the
hour-long TV drama. At the book's conclusion they cite the
inspiring 2002 season of *The West Wing*, where the fictional
President wins reelection "on an Apollo-type clean-energy
investment platform."

Dan wakes groggily and soon we are paddling again across
Cow Island Pond. Hungover after our evening at the Irish

Alehouse, we approach the morning's task like two bleary-eyed galley slaves. Our moods are not aided by the wind, which blows directly in our faces. After twenty minutes of hard paddling, I stare at the shore and swear we are still directly across from the same branch of the same gnarled oak tree. After a while we start to move. Sirens go off as we pass by Millennium Park, providing a strange soundtrack to the beauty surrounding us: black willow trees, a downy woodpecker, and little pink-purple cups of wild petunia. After a good stretch of paddling we reach Nahantan Park. Dan is talking again but the wind blows the boat and his sentences backward. Here in the bow I catch about every third or fourth word. If I am getting what he is saying, the park coming up on our right was once known for its high frequency of homosexual "encounters." The problem reached such proportions that a special city government meeting was called, and Dan was asked to join the group. They should have thought twice before they sent that invitation. Always an innovative thinker—a minor visionary as he himself suggested—Dan had a novel solution: they should create a new park in the city that would provide what Nahantan was already known for. In other words this new park would have a place designated for "encounters." Then everyone would know what was what and if that wasn't your scene you'd move on to another park.

"If the demand is there, you can't end the supply," he argued. "You have to think of it in original ways."

Dan's proposal didn't carry the day.

Another hour of hard paddling follows.

My back hurts and I long for the fancy, comfortable kayak of day one. When I eventually long out loud, Dan tosses me a pillow from his pack, which I place over my

hard seat. A little while later, when I start waxing poetic
about the pillow, he dubs it "Wilson," after Tom Hanks'
famous cinematic volleyball.[15] We don't talk much but focus
on our twin goals of making it down the river and exorcis-
ing our hangovers. No one has yet mentioned that it is our
country's birthday.

As we paddle, I search the sky for birds. Last night,
when we were crossing Cow Island Pond on our way to the
Alehouse I was treated to the site of an osprey hovering above.
It was hard to see at first, but its crooked wings gave it away.
Dan said it was the first one he'd seen on the river. I resisted
any talk about "totem animals" and was happy when he
did, too.

While I have more and more respect for Dan as an environmentalist, when it comes to the English language, he
isn't exactly Thoreau or Carson.

"Fuck yeah!" was his response to seeing the osprey.

Which was better than what it might have been. I'll take
"fuck" over mystical oneness any day of the week. And yet,
while Dan is all grit and common sense talking policy, he
has a pretty romantic way of describing his inspiration.

"Nature tricks you," he said to me as we paddled. "You
fall in love with it and you love it so much that you end up
fighting for it."

It almost sounded chivalrous, as if nature was a maiden
and Dan one of her knights. But if that example treads close
to the mawkish, I don't object to his frequent use of the word
"vision." Slap a "quest" at the end of the word and before you
know it you're talking about drumming and fire-walking, and
it does tread dangerously close to Robert Bly territory. But
in Dan's case, the word choice seems appropriate. That was
what he did after all. He *saw* what the Charles could return

to before other people did, presented others with the picture in his mind, and then, despite all the political fights and setbacks and compromises, he went ahead and made something close to what he had seen manifest itself in the world.

Certainly, that is something important in these compromised, apathetic times. It is, at the very least, a better way of spending one's time on earth than trading stocks or piling up money. It is — and I hope I can say this in the least Disney-like fashion — a hopeful and inspiring way to be.

We paddle hard through the morning until Donna picks us up at the Silk Mill Dam and whisks us ahead, like a lucky roll of the dice in Chutes and Ladders, skipping the upcoming dam-riddled section of the river. She has brought tubs of coffee, bless her, and I am thinking now that she is not such a bad Sherpa after all.

We climb back into the leaky boat near the Duck Feeding launch, about thirteen miles from downtown, at the beginning of the so-called Lake District. Before long, after two quiet days, we are part of a small American flag-waving armada. We pass a family in a canoe, all four of them wearing Red Sox hats, and Dan calls over to see who won last night. As it turns out, all is right in the world and the Sox have beaten Tampa Bay four to one. Obviously, our wild journey is taking a decidedly social turn. Dan describes what the place was like seventy years ago.

"There was an amusement park, a zoo, and a floating drive-in theater that didn't make it because everyone was getting nauseated. There were dozens of canoe liveries along the river. And they even had a jail cell where they locked people up for necking."

He points out that some of that tradition continues as we pass the Charles River Kayak and Canoe Center, which "get hundreds of kids out on river." While other parts of the Charles sneak through peoples' backyards, the Lake District is as obvious, open, and friendly as a yellow lab. It continues to get the most passive, non-motorized boating of the whole river.

"One of my driving ideas is to give the locals access," Dan says as we paddle past Mount Feake Cemetery. "For instance, the Lake district has a long history of ice fishing. A guy pulled out a forty-eight inch, thirty-seven pound northern pike right here in Waltham. But the rules said they couldn't fish and people got kicked off. I fought to get them permits."

"Every chance, you need to let people get on the river. Eliminate the rules and regulations. Let people interact. Don't fence things off."

There is one thing he doesn't want to allow on the river, however. As we paddle into the Lake District, Dan points down at one of his time-sworn enemies.

"Water chestnut," he says. "This shit sucks. One of the most aggressive invasives. It's an escaped aquarium plant. People think nothing of dumping their fish tanks in the river. It gets spread by the propellers of boats and in birds' plumage.

"The best thing about native plants is that they bring back native species. I've tried to plant native plants, but I really don't mind invasives as long as they are blending with other plants. Water chestnut is different. It actually threatens the aquatic ecosystem because of the amount of dissolved oxygen it takes in. It decomposes and can threaten fish life and it's always dangerous if you get caught

up in it in a boat. We've spent about 650,000 dollars battling it over the last seven or eight years. It's been a major
harvesting program. Luckily, it responds well to mechani-
cal harvesting so you don't have to use chemicals."

✕

This stretch of river was deeply influenced by the vision of
someone other than Dan. An area of impounded water
created in part by the Moody Dam downstream, this water
was a celebrated part of Boston life during the early twentieth century, home to Big Band dance halls and thousands
of regular canoeists, a great river community center—just
the kind of spirit Dan is trying to restore. In fact much
of the land that Dan has reclaimed along the Charles was
originally purchased for the state in the late nineteenth
century by the visionary landscape architect Charles Eliot.
Eliot saw the banks of the river as a place for solace from
the ever-growing city, and without that original purchase
there would have been no hope for the present vision.

In the Lake District, Dan's is as much a *revision* as it is a
vision. Much of the land that would become his nature corridors and bike paths, and the banks where he would plant
his native plants, was already owned by the state, thanks
to the efforts of a previous generation of environmental
dreamers, including Eliot, over a hundred years before. In
1893, Boston became the first city in the United States to
create a metropolitan park system, and part of the early
push of the founders of that park system was to purchase,
and claim by eminent domain, the green ribbon along the
banks of the Charles. Over the years, however, the state
ignored its land, and the homeowners and business owners who lived by the river naturally encroached on public

land. It would become Dan's job to pry that land away
from them. And of course to convince them that this was
a good idea.

As Dan points out, human notions about the river have
always had a direct effect on its health. Before Eliot got
to work, the Charles was seen as many rivers were at the
time: a kind of all-natural sewer system that swept your
shit away. In fact, it was an interesting confluence of the
most base, practical need — getting rid of one's crap — and
the most high-minded — the evolving ideas of nature as
a kind of "cathedral" — that came together in late nineteenth century Boston to form America's first metropolitan park system and the first public works commissions
for sewage and water. Both were founded here within six
years of each other, between 1889 and 1893. Born from
the practical consideration of getting water to drink and
getting rid of waste was the possibility of a more romantic
ideal: giving the people in the newly crowded city a place
to get away from it all. Eliot led the charge of a group of
Brahmin reformers in this first greening of Boston. As
Boston historian James C. O'Connell puts it: "This effort
was the urban counterpart to the Progressive campaign
of Theodore Roosevelt, Gifford Pinchot, and others to
preserve natural wonders and rationally manage natural
resources by creating national parks and national forests."[16]

But the river became more than a place to get away; it
was a huge social center. On any given day there were three
thousand canoes for rent, and the river, formerly a place to
dump sewage became a place to congregate, picnic, swim.

Given what we are seeing on July Fourth — dozens of
people out on the river in canoes, kayaks, and powerboats —
you could be forgiven for thinking that this social tradition

has continued unabated from the early twentieth century. But, as O'Connell writes, "When World War II broke out, Boston's metropolitan parks were at a height of popularity they would never see again." After the war the rise of the suburbs, and the car, led to a decline in parks, and funding that had once gone toward green space went toward bombs instead.

The result of those decades that followed was that Bostonians lost their rightful access to the river. Businesses put up chain-link fences and built parking lots to the edge of the water. Imagine if you were living in Waltham forty years ago or so and wanted to get a peek at the water. You might have snuck around a fence and slid down a weedy bank, and all the while you'd be feeling that you were doing something not just dangerous but wrong. Guilt would no doubt accompany your desire to see the city's wet pulse. It would never occur to you that you actually had the legal right to sit there and watch the water.

"Basically, Boston turned its back on the river. Buildings were built as if the river wasn't there and people started dumping again. The human perception of the river changes with time. Each era has its own river. But the fifties through the seventies was the worst period. Part of the demise of the parks was caused by the rise of the suburbs. The dream of having your own piece of nature with a grill and a car you could wax while you grilled. And that altered the public consciousness toward the public open spaces. So we had a collective force going against the river as open space. Everything contributed. It was a time of industrial pollutants and a time that lacked the concern for coming together that was there in the 1920s and 1930s. Fortunately that need has prevailed and it's back again. And now on July Fourth, we're about to paddle into the Mecca of that experience where people are coming together collectively for a huge event. Unfortunately this is a heinous celebration of our war-like ways, but we'll enjoy it."

It wasn't until the late sixties that people, and city planners, kind of started to dimly remember the hidden, watery thing behind their backs. By then the original Metropolitan Park Commission had long since become the Metropolitan District Commission (MDC) and, like its name, had taken on a more practical, and less poetic, bent.[17] For the next couple of decades the organization that was born of Eliot's romantic ideas of "nature as cathedral" transformed into a babysitter for softball fields and ice rinks. But with the environmental awakening of the sixties, and the river's health aided by the Clean Water Act, plans emerged for a return to, and possibly even an expansion of, Eliot's original vision.

"I came along at the right time," Dan admits. "The state economy would go in the shitter again soon. But for a minute there, there was some money. And excitement."

The section that Dan first set out to reclaim is the section that we will be paddling through this afternoon. There the chain-link fences were up, the banks reduced to scrub, the river an afterthought. It was, hands down, the ugliest stretch on the river.

 BIRD MEN

We pull over on a small wooded island next to Quinobequin Cove and sit in the shade below a red maple. Sipping on a Long Trail IPA, I reach into my dry pack and pull out a cigar—a Macanudo—while staring out at the water. We feel better, and not just due to the hair of the dog. The sun slices down through the trees and morning's exertion has lifted the mood. I place Wilson on the roots of the maple and pat him gently before sitting on him while stretching my feet down into the water. Volunteer aspens sway behind us.

For Dan this area is steeped in personal history. Less than a mile, straight across the water, is the house where he lived during the early days of his fight to resuscitate the river.

"That's where I was when I first fought for the reservation," he says, pointing his beer bottle toward Ware's cove. "I moved in there just prior to being assigned this part of the Charles. And that's really the spot where I had my own rediscovery of the river. That's when I bought this canoe."

He looks gratefully at the canoe, perhaps thinking back to its first trips, while realizing this might be its last.

"At first, in those days, I just ran on raw enthusiasm. I didn't know that you weren't supposed to try and do extraordinary things. I'm glad I was naïve, or I wouldn't have started in the first place. I had no idea what kind of fight I was in for."

I ask what it really felt like—during the early years of fighting. I don't get the feel-good answer I expect.

"It sucked," he says, shaking his head. "We had written up a master plan for what we called the Middle Charles River Reservation, but almost everyone was against it. The only people who really supported us were Bob Zimmerman and the Charles River Watershed Association. I went to a meeting in Newton, and 130 residents showed up—all angry and all against the plan. Everywhere people were saying that my paths were going to bring crackheads into their neighborhoods. They said if I built paths by the river they would erect an eight-foot chain-link fence. Then a congressman's office called and tried to stop us. Local officials had told him I was building a motorcycle course on the river, and I had to prove it wasn't true.

"On top of that I was battling my own people within the state bureaucracy. Early on someone wrote a positive article about me in the newspaper. A co-worker came up to me later and said: 'That article really hurt you.' I guess when you work for the state you're not supposed to stand out. I started to mutter to myself, 'Someone get me out of this project.'

"Government's strange. They don't want you to do extraordinary work. They pull you down if you do extraordinary work. You don't get credit, and you're not supposed to get credit. So I don't ever even try to get credit anymore. And still I get flak for getting too much attention, for standing out. I tell them, 'You can go to the press events and get all the credit. If you fund it, I will do it and not take any credit. But if you don't fund me, I'll keep scrambling and keep doing it the way I've been doing it.'"

He stares off downstream. It occurs to me that it is the

first crack in his optimism I've seen in two days. He is quiet
for minute before continuing.

"During those times I'd go down to the river a lot.
Sometimes in those days I'd smoke a little hit of pot and
let the river bring some magic to me, to rejuvenate me and
get me re-motivated to go back into that maze of human
obstacles to make it happen. After the depressing meeting in
Newton I walked out on a bluff above the river. I was angry,
sick of it all. Then, while I was staring out, a black-crowned
night heron landed on a branch near me. Then another and
another until there were twelve or thirteen of them. That
rejuvenated and remotivated me to go back into that maze
of human obstacles to make it happen. Screw humans, I
thought. I'll do it for the animals."

He takes a long pull on his beer.

"That lifted me. To tell you the truth the animals were
my key to support at the beginning. When I wasn't getting a
lot of human support."

Corny? God yes. But what does that matter in the face
of results? Of course, I love the fact that birds were at
the bottom of things. It makes me want to run and find
Shellenberger and Nordhaus, wherever they're hiding, and
tell them that *this* is the way things really work.

Whatever the motivation, Dan kept his birds and mysticism to himself and set about trying to convert both his
neighbors and his neighborhood. The mob he'd faced was
ugly, but he found that his neighbors, as individuals, were
less so. By all accounts it was his affable straightforward-
ness, as well as his stubborn streak, that allowed him to win
over angry residents, like those 130 Newtonians. Often he
would seek out the residents by knocking on their doors

and showing them his plans, inviting them down to the river so he could give them a tour and describe his vision. He did this for three years. And despite the characteristic litigiousness of the American people, the *Boston Globe* would write: "What is remarkable is not that the MDC finally retook its own land, but that it has resolved the vast majority of the encroachments without a single lawsuit."[18]

This was miraculous. People agreeing to give up something they believed was theirs for the common good.

"We kept pushing the idea that the river belonged to the people," Dan says. "That the people could be its stewards."

As it turns out, many of those who opposed the idea are now its greatest backers. So far the paths haven't brought crackheads to Newton. Instead the banks flower with viburnum, berrying shrubs, native blueberries, and white pines, while supporting an ecosystem of increasingly varied animal life: roosting herons, fox, muskrats, white-tailed deer.

$$\times$$

I am trying to be hard-headed and practical in the sort of environmentalism I'm putting forth here, but birds keep getting in the way. I like the fact that Dan's fight was intertwined with birds and in this he doesn't seem too different than many who fight for the wild.

I think back to the osprey flying through the dusk over the Alehouse, and I think of the way ospreys have lifted my life. Again, I'm resisting the idea of a "totem animal," but if I were ever to cave to that groovy notion, the osprey would be mine. Last night's bird rose and hovered, like a muscular hummingbird, decked out in feathers of dark brown and white, and I, looking up, could sense its tension, and yelled to Dan right before it dove. It missed its target but the sport of it was enough, at least for me.

I love the directness of ospreys, the way their whole lives depend on this simple and savage getting of fish. Back on Cape Cod I studied the way they dove: the hover, the reading of the water, the initial dive, the adjustment, the final abandoned plunge, the popping of the last-second wheelie, the stabbing for fish with their great talons.

Birds are my soft spot. Friends mock me for it but I'm a sucker for anything with feathers that flies. In particular, anything that flies with a black bandit mask and that has an insatiable hunger for fish. Ospreys are my weakness. John Muir wrote: "When we try to pick out anything by itself, we find it hitched to everything else in the universe." Ospreys are hitched to the world in unexpected ways.

Large, nearly eagle-sized raptors with five-and-a-half to six foot wingspans, ospreys are known for their swashbuckling dives and are distinguished by their dark brown masks and vivid brown-and-white wing patterns. Before I got to know the birds, I never considered myself much of a birder, let alone an ornithologist. My early encounters with them on Cape Cod were casual, but then I became curious about their behavior and that curiosity gradually transformed into obsession. Watch these birds a while and it's hard not to get excited. The first time I saw an osprey hit the water, after pulling in its wings and hurtling down from fifty feet in the air, I literally jumped for joy. I did this more as a sports fan than a birder, and, like a fan, I immediately wanted to grab someone else and tell them about it: After all, what I had witnessed was supremely athletic. But as well as being spectacular athletes, ospreys are gregarious and extroverted—their open ways seem to invite you into their lives. At some point I took that invitation. I am forever glad I did.

One thing led to another. One fall I decided to follow the migration of some Cape Cod ospreys as they made their

way down the East Coast to Cuba and then down to South
America. There were great pleasures in watching the birds
but these were rivaled in watching the people who watched
the birds. I met dozens of other bird people, my fellow
tribesmen and women, who spent the better part of their
lives studying ospreys. I am not going to make a grand claim
that this somehow made them better people than the rest
of us, but I do think there is something encoded in human
beings that gives us pleasure when we spend a good part of
our time outdoors watching animals. "Joy is the symptom
by means of which right contact can be measured," wrote
Joseph Wood Krutch in his biography of Thoreau. And
there was something joyous about this bird tribe that I had
stumbled upon. Not perfect, not content, not morally superior, just joyous.

It was during this trip that I visited Cuba and met Freddy
Santana Rodriguez. Freddy's life changed one day in 1996
when he discovered a dead male osprey with a band on his
leg in the area near his home in Santiago, Cuba. Through
the information on the osprey's band, Rodriguez got in
touch with Keith Bildstein, the director of conservation
science at Hawk Mountain, a well-known site for watching
raptor migration in Pennsylvania. Freddy's find would lead
to his becoming the first Cuban intern at Hawk Mountain,
and when he got home to his country he would establish a
site for observing migrating ospreys on La Gran Piedra, a
rock outcropping in the Sierra Maestra mountain range
in eastern Cuba. From then on he tied his life to the birds,
and his happiest moments were watching the annual river
of ospreys, shining black and white above, as they flowed
overhead through the mountains each fall. Naturally he
began, not just to study, but to protect the birds; working

to educate his countrymen about them; coming out against
hunting and the destruction of the natural places in Cuba
that served as pit stops on the bird's migratory route. But
the activism came later. First was the joy in seeing the wild
and beautiful athleticism of the birds in flight.

$$\times$$

That's a nice story, you say. But isn't it a bit off point? This is
still a manifesto after all. How is an osprey or some herons
going to SAVE THE WORLD? How are they going to STOP
GLOBAL WARMING?

Well, because everything's hitched to everything else,
let me try another story on you, this one also involving
ospreys. I'll warn you going in that this is the sort of hoary
sixties era environmental chestnut that so grates on the
nerves of the Nordhauses and Shellenbergers of the world.
But I like it. And it fits well, in my mind at least, with
Dan's story and the story of the sort of environmentalism
that appeals to me. It's the story of two friends on Long
Island, Art Cooley and Dennis Puleston. These two start
going bird watching together in the fifties. At that time,
Art is a middle school science teacher — a hearty, energetic young man fresh out of college — and someone tells
him about Dennis, who is already a kind of local legend
who has sailed around the world, written books, and, during World War II, invented the famous amphibious duck
boats. "Oh, you're interested in birds," another friend
says to Art, "then you've got to meet Dennis Puleston."

Dennis, it turns out, is an osprey freak. He is also an
artist, and one of the subjects for his art are the ospreys
that he observes regularly on Gardiners Island, off the
northern end of Long Island. After Dennis and Art have

gone out birding a couple times on the weekend, heading, with binoculars in hand, to some marsh or beach or
woods, they notice they have a lot of extra room in the
car, and, being natural educators, they start inviting along
kids from Art's middle school, teaching them about birds.
They do this pretty regularly until Art goes off to fight in
Korea, and then when he gets back, they start up again.

By this time — it's the early sixties now — Art has gotten
a job as a high school biology teacher and Dennis has begun
to notice that the osprey population on Gardiners Island
is plummeting. Then Dennis reads Rachel Carson's *Silent
Spring* and it's all over. His mind starts buzzing with connections. Carson explains how DDT, sprayed to kill insects,
has permeated ecosystems with deadly results, especially
for animals, like the osprey, on the top of the food chain.

A couple of more year pass and Art is teaching a ma-
rine science class. He teaches this class at the high school
but also, to help make ends meet, he teaches it as an adult
education course, and in both courses he always uses local
issues to illustrate his points. In the night school class, he
has the students chart how duck farms pollute Long Island
Sound. Then he takes the class to Mt. Sinai Harbor where
Art points out the dredging that has been going on — pretty
common stuff in those days — wetlands dug up and the
muck from the marshes, the fill, dumped to create land to
build houses on. Art bemoans this practice, but leaves it at
that, at least until the next night when a student from the
class calls him at home.

The student has been talking to another student and
they have a question for Art. "What are you going to
do about this?" they ask Art. "What are you going to *do*
about the duck farms and the dredging?" Well, it's a good

question. Art teaches full time, and he teaches the night
school class, and of course he's got a wife and kids, too, and
it really isn't his job to save the world. But he starts asking
questions and one thing leads to another. The two adult
students get involved, and so does Dennis Puleston, his bird-
watching partner, and then some other people do too.

Which is to say that Art does something very important. He forms a *group*. It's hard to express how much this
changes things. Individuals, artists like Rachel Carson for
instance, might bring back something, a vision, a book,
that inspires. But groups get things done. This group
has a name (the Brookhaven Town Natural Resources
Committee or BTNRC) and annual dues (one dollar per
year for mimeographing) and Art is elected chairman. Art,
it turns out, has a talent for running the meetings, maybe
learned in his years of teaching high school students; he
is burly with a deep voice, good at telling people to shut
up and get started, and also at summarizing what they've
discussed and then assigning people tasks to get done by
the next time the group meets. It's a surprisingly effective
strategy: Tell yourself that you will get something done
and you may, but there is no one to report back to. That
is quite different than reporting back to a group, specifically to a man as big and forceful as Art Cooley, and saying, "Um . . . sorry, I failed." The word people from that
time often used to describe Art is "energetic," but "tough"
gets in there fairly often, too. You didn't want to come
back to Art and tell him you didn't get your job done.

Different words are used to describe Dennis Puleston,
for instance "gentle" and "brilliant"—but that is the beauty
of a group: it can contain multitudes. Different people bring
different skills to the party. Other group members include

George Woodwell, head ecologist at Brookhaven National
Laboratory, and Charles Wurster, a biology professor at
Stony Brook University and an expert on chemical pesticides. But to ignite these more serious scientific personalities, a spark is needed. Art, with his energy and bouncer's
brawn, provides the organizational spark, but another spark
comes uninvited in the personage of Victor Yannacone, a
flamboyant local lawyer.

It is said of Yannacone that "the only thing silent about
him was the final 'e' in his name," and when he reads a local
editorial written by Wurster, decrying the use of the chemical DDT in spraying local marshes, he wastes no time filing
a suit against the local Mosquito Commission, the sprayers
of the chemical. Yannacone then approaches the BTNRC,
and it is here that the individual talents of the group came
to the fore. "Do you have any evidence?" Yannacone asks.
Well, yes, it turns out they do. Dennis Puleston draws on
his studies of the Gardiners Island ospreys, where he has
been noting the number of nests and birth rates, and where
only fifty nests remain from the original three hundred he
began studying. In fact there are only three chicks this year,
and from the failed nests he brings the too-thin eggshells to
Charles Wurster's lab, where Wurster confirms they contain DDT. George Woodwell, not to be outdone, writes a
brilliant paper on biomagnification, describing the process
by which DDT rises up the food chain, increasing in toxic-
ity in larger species. In court Yannacone presses the point
that the chemical is threatening the community, and Art
Cooley testifies in his usually emphatic manner. Dennis
Puleston provides beautiful drawings of ospreys, and his
charts of the falling osprey population are exhibit A, which
means that the osprey, hitched to everything, finds itself

smack in the middle of the country's first cases of what
will soon come to be known as "environmental law."

Things speed up after that. The judge delays but then
agrees to grant a stay that stops the Mosquito Commission
from spraying. In the meantime public opinion turns against
DDT, and the local extermination companies bow to public
pressure, switching to more organic pesticides. When the
judge's decision comes back, months later, he decides not
to decide, acknowledging the danger of DDT but saying it
is not in his powers to judge, an issue for the legislature. By
then it doesn't matter. Art and company are off and running.
There is a wonderful moment in any project, any great effort, when impotence transforms into potency. When an individual, or group, suddenly realizes, "Hey, I actually can do
something. . . . I can impact the world." This is why Derrick
Jensen and the anti-hope gang are dead wrong. Suddenly "I
did something" transforms into "I can do more?!" Suddenly
momentum takes over and energy surges.

"What you've got to understand is that we were all
friends," Art will say later, trying to explain the intoxicated
mood of the time. "We all *liked* each other. Many of us were
naturalists and birders. For years we had felt pushed around
by big companies, the chemical people. And suddenly we
realized that we might actually be able to push back. It was
terrifically exciting."

There are some within the BTNRC who feel they have
done enough, but there are others who believe they are
just getting started. Those others—including Art, Dennis
Puleston, George Woodwell, Charles Wurster, and Victor
Yannacone—form another group, which they called the
Environmental Defense Fund. The EDF is incorporated as
a nonprofit organization with a mission to "encourage and

support the conservation of the natural resources of the United States of America." The first thing the group does is file a suit against the Michigan Department of Agriculture, trying to stop the spraying of DDT and the use of pesticides around Lake Michigan. That case is thrown out on a technicality, but the next case, in neighboring Wisconsin, is not. Thanks to the Environmental Defense Fund, DDT is soon banned in that state. A few years later, in June of 1972, the chemical will be banned throughout the country by the newly formed Environmental Protection Agency. People will point to both the Environmental Defense Fund and the writing of Rachel Carson as prime movers behind this law.

If there was a sense of momentum after the Long Island court case, imagine the sense after Wisconsin, or after the national ban. Imagine the sense of "we did something" transforming into "let's do more!" Imagine the ice breaking and the floes beginning to steam downstream. Oh, and remember, by the way, it began with *bird watching*.

Today Art Cooley sounds positively jolly when he recounts the EDF's motto, at least their private motto, during those heady days.

Their motto was this: "Sue the bastards."

 ANTAEUS

Sue the bastards!

Think of the life in those words. So much better than "The World is Doomed." Even if it is.

The proof, as they say, is in the pudding. As with the results of Dan's fight—the green banks we have been paddling by—the results of Art Cooley's and Dennis Puleston's are there for anyone to see. For the ospreys, the effects of the DDT ban were immediate and dramatic: the coast quickly filled again with brown-and-white wings and wild, shaggy nests. In 1960, thirteen pairs of ospreys nested in Massachusetts while today we have well over three hundred. But the story itself is as important as the results. In the face of the familiar litany of environmental pessimism—not just global warming but depleted resources and the intractable crush of population—it is easy to close down. But I am energized by the fact that a few people took action and actually affected change, or, to put it another way, it is thanks to the fact that some Long Islanders sued the bastards that we now have ospreys on Cape Cod.

I believe that the osprey story, like Dan's story, is worth repeating in these embattled times. It seems a vital puzzle piece as I try to fit together my own green philosophy. One lesson, arguably the biggest lesson, we can take from it is how small, local change can have large, global results. "It all began in our backyard," is how Art Cooley recently put it. And it ended as one of the biggest and most successful environmental organizations of the twentieth century. Of course the technocrats would love to put Art's story permanently on the shelf with the rest of the cobwebbed old stuff. They would prefer to replace it with a "vision of affluence."

For my part I don't get excited by the idea of humans turning into a band of chipper entrepreneurs. "The life which men praise and regard as successful is but one kind," said Thoreau.[19] A great life can be a different life, a new life. For the last thirty years we have told ourselves tales of affluence without sacrifice, of big cars and big houses—but there are other stronger, deeper myths that can guide us in the future which have also guided us in the past.

In a quest for newer, shinier ways to save the world, influenced, no doubt, by our belief that we can Google our way to any solution, we forget that stories matter. They may be chestnuts, but Dennis Puleston and Art Cooley's story, and Dan Driscoll's story for that matter, are ones that should be told and re-told, repeated around campfires. We don't need more theory, disembodied from the world. We need stories, told outside, told in a way that links activism to beauty, wild beauty. (And yes, there are beautiful places, countless beautiful places, near Boston and on Long Island—still.) They should be told in the open air so that we remember that loving and fighting aren't two specialties, but one thing, or at least two things that are part of a whole, connected through the pumping blood of a single circulatory system.

I can see why Nordhaus and Shellenberger consider Art Cooley's story outdated. For one thing it starts with Rachel Carson. *Oh god not Rachel Carson again*, you hear them moaning, *please not again.* . . . The Carson model, remember, is that of an artist retreating to nature, then returning with a vision and that vision influencing the world. For another it fits what Nordhaus and Shellenberger call "the pollution paradigm," the old model of environmental-ism that they claim we will all have to give up now that we are fighting a new fight against a colorless, odorless gas in this age of global warming. But it could be that what they like least of all about the story is the simple fact that a large national fight, a fight with global consequences, began as a local battle over disappearing ospreys and some duck crap in a few Long Island ponds.

Because, to put it as simply as possible, Nord and Shell don't get places. Yes, it's true, believe it or not. They like the world, or at least they claim to, but local places, actual neighborhoods or street corners or copses of trees with squirrels in them strike them as, well, kind of yucky. You can see them up there on the shiny, clean bridge of the *Enterprise*, Kirk and Spock, or maybe, in their case, Spock and Spock, gazing placidly at a planet on the view screen but never quite wanting to beam down and leave their antiseptic ship.

For these two Spocks, one of the great culprits of mod-ern environmentalism, one of the reasons it needs to die, is NIMBY-ism, or the famous "Not-In-My-Backyard" syndrome.

For an example of why fighting for one's backyard is so bad they point to a battle that has been raging for almost a decade in my former home. The controversy began when an entrepreneur named Jim Gordon proposed satisfy-ing the Cape's ever-increasing energy needs by erecting 130 wind turbines out in Nantucket Sound, and the issue

gained national prominence for the usual Cape Cod reason: As it turned out the wind farm, as it came to be called,
would be in the Kennedys' watery backyard, and the family
trumpeted and harrumphed about this. Cape residents
were split on the issue and I, a Cape resident, was split too,
unsure what was right. But Nordhaus and Shellenberger,
looking down from outer space, were not split. Of course
they had good points to start with. Yes, Robert Kennedy
was a hypocrite for supporting wind power everywhere
but where he could see it (though he is clearly one of Dan
Driscoll's good "fighting hypocrites," having done much
to clean up the Hudson and other rivers), and, yes, we of
course needed to start exploring alternative energy. The
problem, you see, isn't that Nordhaus and Shellenberger
support Cape Wind, which is something that I, and most
Cape Codders, have also ultimately come to do. The problem is that they, as usual, go too far, taking Cape Wind as
their jumping off point to blame NIMBY-ism for all that is
wrong with environmentalism. According to the authors,
caring about one's backyard is synonymous with small
thinking, an irrational prejudice comparable to racism.

Yes, they really say this: "We no longer believe it is justified to confine our affections to or reserve our loyalties for
a particular race. Why then do we believe we are justified
in reserving our loyalties for a particular place?" The real
problem, according to the dynamic duo, is good old "place-
based environmentalism," and those narrow-minded,
old-fashioned "place-based" environmentalists who fight
for their own places.

True, NIMBY-ism can certainly be narrow-minded and
class-based, but, far from being a snobby evil, it is actually where a lot of environmentalism is born. Think Dan

Driscoll. Think Art Cooley and the beginnings of the EDF.
Think of Diane Wilson, the down-on-her-luck shrimper who
went from being just another fisherwoman to singlehand-
edly fighting off multinational chemical companies because
they fucked with her backyard: the Gulf of Mexico. What
Nord and Shell neglect is the fact that almost all environmentalism grows out of places, and that most of it grows out
of home places. As I mentioned earlier, my own first small
burst of activism came when a trophy house was built, quite
literally, in my backyard. If you aren't going to fight for your
home you aren't very likely to fight for any place. And if you
don't have a connection to a particular place, and to particular animals, humans and otherwise, who dwell in that place,
then you don't fight. It's that simple. The Spock twins argue
just the opposite. We need to think of policy not place. We
need to think internationally, not locally, and we are bigots if
we favor one place over another.

If they and their ilk don't like place, then please oh please
don't talk to them about actual animals. When Jim Gordon
first introduced the idea of erecting wind turbines off the
coast, I was at the height of my love affair with Cape Cod.
Like a lot of people I was more than a little apprehensive
about what the turbines might do to the birds. Furthermore,
I had some scary insider information. My work with ospreys
had led to my getting to know two Scottish ornithologists
who worked as consultants to wind farms in Europe.

"The machines don't do too much damage unless they
are in migratory routes," they told me, off the record. "But
put them in migratory routes and they can kill a lot of
birds." And Cape Cod is dead in the middle of one of the
world's biggest migratory routes: A million birds a night
migrate over the peninsula at the height of the fall season.

But when Nordhaus and Shellenberger consider this issue from the deck of the *Enterprise*, anxieties about migrating birds and other wildlife are quickly and easily dismissed. They write: "Studies of wind turbines in Europe similar to the ones that are planned for Cape Wind have found vanishingly few bird deaths annually." *Vanishingly few!* Whatever the fuck that means. If one follows the footnote of this statement it will lead to two sources, one a BBC news report and the other an article in a local glossy tourist magazine, *Cape Cod Today*. This is in line with their other research. For instance, countering Robert Kennedy's extensive early objections to the wind farms, the authors write: "Indeed we were able to debunk most of them in just forty-five minutes of fact-checking on Google and the Nexus news database." Apparently the line is written without irony.

As for the birds and animals of Nantucket Sound, they are reduced to a minor role in the drama. It's about saving the world, after all, not saving birds. They quickly dismiss worries about local wildlife, referring to them as "photogenic animals." Any claimed concern with non-human life, after all, is part of the old fashioned "grand environmental narrative" and not *au courant*. This makes sense within their overall logic since individual animals, including human animals, are all of and from a place. That is, they grow some*where*. The trouble again is that without knowledge of particular creatures that live in particular places, it is hard to actually care.

In the end, after much soul-searching and teeth gnashing, I came out in support of the Cape Wind project. I did so after meeting and walking the beach with Jim Gordon, and

I did so with anxiety about the animals and worries for the water, and with fears that I was acting as an avian Judas. And finally I did so hoping that I was not merely being swayed by the times and our current wind-mania. In short, after a lot of brooding, I decided that the wind machines were the best of some bad choices. It is, after all, a time of tough choices, and common sense dictates that some of our eco-choices aren't going to be "pure" ones. But I also supported the wind farm knowing that each place must start to make an accounting of the energy it uses and have an awareness of where that energy comes from. As with so many things, better that it comes from close to home.

So, if I have come to the same conclusion as Nordhaus and Shellenberger, why all the fuss? Other than coming around more slowly, and grudgingly, how am I any different? Well, for one thing, it has been a hard decision. For another it has been a *grounded* decision.

I, for one, don't think my love of one place makes me a racist. In fact I believe that it is precisely my love of place that allows me to think deeply about non-local issues. Nordhaus and Shellenberger write: "Those who have a hard time accepting, nay (nay?), *embracing* windmills in Nantucket Sound or high-rise buildings in urban centers will not be able to create a politics capable of helping countries like China (not to mention the United States) meet their energy needs in a more ecologically sound way." Well that's easy for them to say. But while the national media portrayed anyone who opposed Cape Wind as a Thurston Howell the Third wearing pants with whales on them who only cared that the wind turbines would spoil the view during the regatta, the truth was more complicated. The truth was that many of us wrestled with the issue, and that

wrestling was just another way of being deeply involved
with one's home. My old backyard is a complicated place
and it includes Buzzards Bay where I have seen wind's
alternative, oil, cover the wings of shorebirds during a
recent spill. The decision on whether or not to support Jim
Gordon may be easy from the outside but from within it is
a hard decision, made harder and more complex by local
knowledge. From the great heights of placelessness it's
easy to smooth over the complexities of an issue that, like
all issues, even global warming, is local as well as global.

In the end any talk of policy must incorporate this sort
of local knowledge or be, of necessity, disconnected and
brittle. Yes, policy is important, indisputably important.
But what is policy other than shackles if it does not come
from some place, and speak to the particular people rooted
in that place? Is it really possible to have sweeping environmental changes without acknowledging that you are an
animal that comes from a particular animal territory? Is
it possible to have policy that ignores this or that ignores
the other animals you happen to share your place with?

The most startling thing about Cape Wind was not that
people behaved so badly but that so many Cape citizens, in
the end, thought out and fought out the issue, and ended
up supporting the project. That is they decided, finally, that
we must provide our own power and that it is worth seeing
where that power comes from.

I support the wind project, but due to my fear for the
birds I still do so reluctantly. Perhaps I should more enthusi-
astically accept—*nay, embrace!*—the wind farm. But for the
moment the best I can do is back it.

In a way, Dan Driscoll's story is the opposite of NIMBY-ism, since, ultimately, he ended up trying to take people's backyards from them. But he wouldn't have been involved in the fight in the first place if he hadn't fallen for his own backyard. Perhaps the larger point is that there is nothing wrong with our environmental ethic beginning in our own backyards—just as long as it doesn't end there.

I believe that Nordhaus and Shellenberger are making a grave mistake when they try to separate environmentalists from the ground they walk on. I still say that a fighter for the earth, new model or old, must have some rooted attachment to the earth he or she is fighting for. Consider, for instance, the way that Nordhaus and Shellenberger end their book by turning to Greek legend. It isn't that the legend they choose to allude to is strange, just the *way* they use it.

They break out the oft-repeated story of the inventor Daedalus, who created wings for his son Icarus, and then warned the boy not to fly too close to the sun. As most of us know, Icarus does just that, and the wax that held his wings together melts so that he crashes down into the ocean and a watery death. The story is usually told to warn of hubris, but Shellenberger and Nordhaus see it differently. In their version Icarus is the chipper new eco-entrepreneur, daring to dream, someone who represents "the aspiration to imagine new realities, create new values, and reach new heights of human possibility." Hubris, it turns out, is not so bad. We need it if we are to "overcome our lower needs and values" and transform into our gleaming new selves.

Why do their sentences, and sentiments, make me so uneasy? Why does it make me want to launch a defense of my own "lower needs"? It could be because down here on planet Earth we get uncomfortable with talk about the perfectibility of humankind. Maybe they're right. Maybe we can be shiny and new . . . maybe we can change and reform . . . maybe. But maybe not.

One of the more basic problems with using Icarus as an environmental model, as a *story*, it seems to me, is that he ends up plunging to his death. But that isn't the only problem. There's also the fact that it was his ambition, quite similar to the authors', to leave the messy earth behind. He wants to fly up above it all and look down at the world as if it were a map.

They can have their myth. I'll stick with another one. Not Icarus, but an old school myth, favored by many before me: Antaeus, son of Poseidon and Gaia. Why Antaeus? The reason his myth has long appealed, and continues to appeal, is not because of who he was (a somewhat murderous giant) but because of the source of his strength. While Icarus flew toward the sun, Antaeus drew his power from the ground. He could not be defeated in battle as long as his feet kept contact with the earth. It's true he was ill-tempered and that he was eventually lifted off the ground and crushed by Hercules. But the point remains. He was only strong when he was rooted. That, to me, seems a better myth for our current battles. Better, I think, to keep in contact with this sloppy earth than to aspire to fly above it.

 ISLAND BOYS

One thing I'm trying to do in this little book is to tell Dan Driscoll's story. But through that story, I'm also trying to explore the idea of being an environmentalist in a new light. I'll come right out and admit that this book is aimed squarely away from anyone that feels certainty about their place in the world and squarely toward those people on the cusp of adulthood who are scratching their chins and wondering just how they should spend the next fifty years or so of their lives. It has been my experience that people often get ideas stuck in their heads pretty early on, and spend many years following those ideas. What I am trying to suggest, what Dan's story suggests, is that they don't have to be purists, prophets, or righteous believers. Their fight can be intertwined with the things they are fighting for—the things that they love, or the things that bring them joy—that is that they, like their heroes, might actually spend some time in the woods, or in the mountains or on the rivers or by the sea. That they might have some fun, believe in some legends, fall in love, and then fight, joyously, for what's good in their world. This is not a trite greeting card sentiment. It is a way to see and be part of what we are fighting for. And what we will see, I think, is that we are not fighting for an energy policy or even a wilderness bill, though we are certainly fighting for those things too. What we are really fighting for, I want to suggest, is something irrational, something deep and wordless, something at odds with what we consider "goals," both our own and society's.

Dan and I are reluctant to leave our little island. We know we need to push off soon but still we sit. I finish my cigar and crack another beer. It is July Fourth, and though we have a profound story to tell you, at the moment we are content to be just two partying Massachusetts guys. Maybe it's wrong to revel in this fact in this day and age, but revel we do. We toast and clink bottles and smoke and rant. We are too old to be doing this, we understand, but we do it anyway.

We settle back on our respective chairs, me on my pillow — Wilson — and Dan on his soil — unnamed — and talk leisurely. Of course we have been talking for the last two days, but a lot of it has been shouting from bow to stern or stern to bow. Now we let things unravel.

We talk about Boston for a while and my desire to move back here, and then we find ourselves talking about Boston accents in movies, which it turns out, is a joint pet peeve.

"Who do you think has the worst Boston accent of all time?" I ask.

"I don't know. There are so many bad ones."

I nominate Robin Williams from *Good Will Hunting*.

"Oh, yah, he was the worst. And he won a fucking Academy Award!"

The conversation wends onward from there. We start talking Ultimate Frisbee, a sport about which our regrets are exactly opposite: Dan's that he hadn't started playing when he was younger, and mine that I had committed too much of my life to it, wasting my twenties and my early thirties hurling myself into a sport many found ridiculous, and trying to win a national championship, which kept eluding me.

We should get going, we really should. But we babble on.

$$\times$$

For the last couple of days I have been throwing around the word "wild" quite a bit. But during our paddle I've also been thinking about what the hell it really means. Dan, for instance, works for the state, hardly a wild profession. And as for me, I'm no wild man. Or, at the very least, my wildness is of a mild variety. I do not roam the woods naked, spear in hand, a pelt covering my loins. I go for walks and I bird-watch a little. I prowl a limited wild and I prowl it with a limited wildness. But this, too, I find encouraging in a way, the fact that, despite all my timidity, I can still receive, in return for mild exertion, so many wild moments. By wild I don't mean an extra tequila shot (though certainly that doesn't hurt now and then) or cracking stupid jokes. I mean, quite simply, regularly reaching out to a world that involves lives-other-than-human and doing so in a way that entails some physical contact with the world (not just watching Animal Planet).

I don't want to overstate the meaning of Dan walking down to the river and seeing the herons when he felt defeated, but I do think it is important. If I am ever going to cobble these stray thoughts into a green manifesto, then I will need to include Dan's herons. But manifestos are meant to be prescriptive, and, if I were to complete one, what would I prescribe? Explore your territory, I've said already. What else? "First, be a good animal," said Ralph Waldo Emerson. Look at the nonhuman creatures in your neighborhood. Go for walks now and again, walks when, for at least short periods, you think about things other than your private ambitions and your things-to-do list. Try brief experiments in caring about the world. And what else? Well, I have to admit that, for all my protestations of modesty, my ambitions for wildness are slightly wider and deeper. In his book *The Abstract Wild*, Jack Turner explains Doug Peacock's rituals among the grizzly bears as follows: they are an "attempt to fill a void in our traditions, an attempt to integrate the wild and the self by myth." Turner sensibly admits that Peacock is "not a shaman" and admits that he lacks a tradition for his rituals, but the deeper point is one worth considering.[20]

Now, it is not wise to wander into mystic caves unless armed with a working bullshit-detector, and yet . . . and yet, I can't help but wander in. So many of even the most basic traditions have been left behind long ago, and any tradition related to wildness was likely left behind long before that. Maybe this is why people like Nordhaus and Shellenberger have such a hard time connecting with place or animals, we're all so afraid of mysticism we can't see that a tradition of wildness doesn't have to be mumbo jumbo. It can just be checking in, seeing how the animals are doing, how our home is doing. I can't help but try to create some ritual in my life and so, while I'm not a religious man, I do observe one holiday quite religiously. Every year on the summer solstice I try to get out to the beach, or to the woods or mountains.

Though I am middle aged now, and though I have a little child, and though my wife does not like spending nights in our house alone, I often spend solstice nights in a tent my parents gave me twenty-five years ago, a

tent named, poetically "Clip Flashlight." I don't do this
because I think camping is morally superior to sleeping
in a bed and I don't do it because I have attained "post-
affluence," whatever that is. I do it because I find that the
summer solstice is a day that is more extraordinary than
other days. Not simply because it is the longest day of the
year—though that is important—but because it is the day
of each year when the sun stops its progression into the
northern sky and the one day I reliably spend the better
part of outdoors (and then spend the night that way too).

For years I would camp out on conservation land near
the bluff on Cape Cod and walk along the shore. One
of the joys of that solstice walk was the way it always
united the non-human and human wild: a mile up the
beach from where I camped I could see the flames of a
fire, the Day family's annual solstice bonfire. The first
year I'd done the walk on solstice, over a decade before,
I'd stumbled upon their fire, a cocktail party appearing right in the middle of a nature walk. In the years
after, stopping there became a tradition. I would inter-
rupt my trek to drink the Day family beer and eat their
steamers and roast their marshmallows, and to learn
who had died, who had married, who had been born.
Afterward I would always stumble back to my tent
in the dunes, all the better for the human contact.

A few years ago I moved to the South and felt a deep
pain at being separated from the place I cared most about.
But the pain has lessened as I've sought out old rituals in
my new place. Last June I spent solstice on an island called
Masonboro, a half-hour paddle from my new house. It
was one of the first times I felt truly at home in my new
world. I sat on the beach and looked toward the west,

toward sunset, toward where my wife and daughter slept.
As I say, I'm no wild man but I felt pretty wild that night.
And pretty joyful. I drank a beer, cold from the small cooler
I packed in the hold of the kayak, and glanced at the sun
going down, figuring twenty minutes left of the long day.
But I didn't care—at the moment I was more interested
in the sea oats waving in front of me, still months from
the husky brown of fall, looking green and fecund as an
early summer wheat field. I got up and headed from the
marsh side of the island to the ocean, a trip that at high tide
takes all of two minutes. Now I walked along the flat hard
sand near the water, still able to see the flooded marshes
but kept immediate company by the ocean, walking to
the rhythm of its beautiful, monotonous roar and slide.

The Atlantic may not be the most romantic of oceans,
but it's the ocean I know best and have known from the
beginning. I passed the charred remains of a fire and
thought that I might or might not make my own solstice
fire. Whether or not I did, I knew I'd likely have a less than
comfortable sleep on the sand. But sleep wasn't the point of
being here. This walk was. The fact that I was noticing the
mobs of dragonflies that hovered in clouds above the elder
bushes. The fact that I had seen oystercatchers and black
skimmers on the paddle over and an osprey with a huge
fish dangling from its talons. The fact that I would still get
a swim in before I circled back to the tent to eat the turkey
sandwich I'd made earlier. The fact that though I knew
I would die soon enough—just like most of the men in
my family (prostate cancer? Heart attack?)—and though I
have been told, but don't quite believe, that the planet will
die, too, I was, for one moment at least, feeling joyful and

goofy and downright happy about being out in the world. What I felt like was a lucky man, my luck coming in almost exact proportion to the days and nights I spent like this.

It's corny, it's romantic, it's hokey. It's not very meta- or modern. But it is the truth.

Earlier in the spring I had paddled out to Masonboro with a friend who is a writer, a modern self-conscious writer, a sometimes meta-writer, a depressed writer who sees the cynical in most everything. As we paddled out to a field of egrets that bloomed like long-stalked, white flowers, all the post- and all the meta- and at least some of the depression went away. Is this because he is, like the rest of us, a romantic fool whose thoughts get mushy around birds and trees? Or is it something deeper? Something encoded in human beings, something that kicked in as he stared at the egrets and said, "Sure the rest of it is bullshit, but this, this island, this place, these birds, this is not bullshit." I don't know for sure that it is the latter. But I'm betting on it.

I was about to say, "I'm betting on it because it is all I've got." But that isn't true. I've got friendship; I've got family; I've got the love of my wife and daughter. And I've got my daily work. But beyond things familial and professional, I think what I have is what we are calling nature. I think what I have is what I've had every solstice for the last couple of decades, whether I was hiking into the Colorado foothills or the dunes of Cape Cod or strolling out along a flat barrier island in North Carolina. I think I've got something other than me, bigger than me, better than me. I don't think this thing I've got is going to make me immortal; I don't think it's going to get me into heaven; and I don't think that it is going to erase my daily anxieties; I don't think it is going to make me a "winner." But I do think it is enough. I do think this thing—let's call it the world for lack of a better term—has given me a great gift, and that the least I can do, once a year or so, is to celebrate it in return.

 DAN'S RIVER

Finally we push off from our little island and paddle into Waltham, the site of Dan's earliest success story. We approach Prospect Street and pass the Waltham Watch Factory, which at one time manufactured the majority of the watches in the US. Dan talks about building a walkway in front of the factory.

"It would be stunning," he says. "Cantilevering over the river."

Unlike the farmlands, quaint villages, and rolling suburbs we have paddled through, Waltham was, from the start, an industrial town. As well as the watch factory, this was the home of the Boston Manufacturing Company, established in 1813. It was here—not in the more famous Lowell mills—that a factory system was established and here that "Mill Girls" lived in dorms and worked eighty hours a week. This was ground zero for Massachusetts' transformation from a farming community to an industrial one. The Charles provided both the power and the dumping grounds for this growth.

Dan points to the other bank.

"On the left here is Nova Biomedical, the first commercial property where we replanted native species. That was the biggest eyesore on the whole river. There was a parking lot right to the edge of the water. Now it's a restored wetlands and everything's thriving, a true habitat—from a parking lot to a complex ecosystem.

"There was this one guy, Fred Spaziani, who worked at Nova, and when everyone else at Nova was against it, Fred really believed in it and fought hard for it. Fred died of cancer, but his leadership was really invigorating and helped get this through. The result was that we reclaimed this, the longest half-mile where there was no public ownership. We got a gift from Nova and then we bought the next section off the MBTA."

As we pull over to portage through downtown Waltham, Dan warns me that we will not be able to leave our bags and equipment and make two trips.

"We're in the city now," Dan says.

As if on cue, two young Hispanic men come strolling up the bike path, just the sort the casual profiler might fear. But I, perhaps buoyed by the beer and cigar, decide to treat their arrival as an opportunity.

"Can you guys give us a hand?" I ask as they walk up, and, before they can think to say no, they find themselves helping us portage our hundred pound boat for the next five hundred yards through the streets of downtown Waltham. We talk as we carry the boat together. Wilson and Juan are both unemployed, or at least they thought they were until this minute, and as they walk they tell us that their parents moved here from Guatemala, and that they were born in the building next to Dan's restored wetlands. In my bad Spanish I start to try to explain that my pillow is also named Wilson, but give up fairly quickly. We wait for the light at a crosswalk and cut down the opposite bank behind the historic Moody Street Mill, kicking a shopping cart out of the way before carrying the boat down a steep dirt path to the water. Before we climb back in the boat, Dan hands Wilson a twenty for the work.

Below the dam we come into the thick of it. Many of

the places upstream bear Dan's mark, or at least are sites
for future plans, but it is here, on this once-grim eight mile
stretch of water running through the grit of Waltham,
Newton, and Watertown, that Dan's dreams of giving
people contact with the river have come to fruition. He
points out spots on the bank as if they were events in his
life—which of course they were.

This stretch was where he first came with survey crews
and old maps and learned almost immediately that the land
that would be his green path had been claimed by encroachment. He had to knock on doors and make phone calls
and try to convince homeowners that property that they
thought was theirs was in fact not.

"Were they pissed off?" I ask.

"Life-threatening," he says. "The local godfather said,
'Don't mess with my people.'"

He points at another building that we glimpse through
the trees.

"These guys had a hundred-car parking lot—an illegal
encroachment. They fought me tooth and nail at first but
now they love it. They have a full maintenance agree-
ment—they offer to take care of their part of the river for
us. They have their meetings out here. Encroachers have
now become stewards. They just couldn't see it before. All
they could see was a wasteland. They said, 'This isn't going
to work.' I had to sell them on the vision."

A little farther along he points again.

"With these corporate landowners, Stop & Shop
in particular, there was really good internal support
for our project. Stop & Shop gifted us two and a half
acres of critical land. This next one we had to buy—this
piece of land here—but the next two were also gifted.
I had a number of successful negotiations with these

corporations. We of course were coming in and cleaning up pretty neglected land. And they had conservation
easements so they still owned the beach. So I think it was
put together in a way that was pretty positive for them.

"Note the houses to the right. We had to switch sides
because of this private property. We would have had to do
a land taking. This used to all be parkland but it was given
away when it shouldn't have been. And it would have been
hard to do a residential land-taking. So that's when I decided
to create the bridge and cross over the river."

We cross under a delicate suspension footbridge. The
140-foot bridge was one of Dan's crowning achievements,
connecting the paths of Newton to Watertown/Waltham.
Dan knew right away what he would call it. The usual
protocol would be to name it after some dead politician.
But Dan called it the Blue Heron Bridge.

One of the first times I met Dan, at least in a non-Frisbee
setting, was during the early days of the construction of
the Blue Heron Bridge. The supports were in but the span
was not, and underpinnings of the bridge had just begun
to jut out over the river. I remember that day because
the rains had been heavy and the river looked truly wild.
We walked west of the bridge behind the Super Stop &
Shop on land that had until just a year before been a land-
fill. But that day you could have easily imagined yourself
next to a river in the mountains during snowmelt. Eddies
over-spilled the banks into a forested flood plain of newly
planted silver maples, and the water swallowed parts of the
path where we stood. The river was loud enough to make
conversing hard.

The Charles had come alive and so had Dan. It was the
first time he spoke to me about his fight to save the river

banks. We circled back to the bridge and he told me that
it — the bridge itself — had proved a puzzle piece that had
solved a seemingly intractable puzzle.

"Homeowners on the Newton side didn't want the path
to go behind their backyards," he said. "They stopped my
path dead in its tracks and I was almost to the point of giving up."

Dan had been stymied for a while before he hit upon
the solution. *A bridge!* Why not cross over into Watertown
and Waltham? Of course it wasn't that easy. First he would
have to talk the corporate folks at Stop & Shop, on the
Watertown side of the river, into gifting two and half acres
of critical land. But once they agreed he was back in business. His path could now run down one side of the river,
cross the Blue Heron Bridge, and then continue wending
eastward.

"Right there you're in Newton — half way across the
bridge you're in Watertown — and then another hundred
and fifty yards to the west and you're in Waltham. So the
Blue Heron Bridge is definitely bridging communities.
And the Newton residents, many of whom opposed it, now
celebrate it and walk across the bridge to shop at Russo's
supermarket and Stop & Shop. Bringing their Newton
money into Waltham and Watertown, which I love."

Today the bridge is in full use: people chatting and
kids with balloons and bike riders zipping across between
Newton and Watertown. On the same bridge Dan once
came upon a woman spreading her father's ashes. She told
him that her father had lived his whole life in Watertown
and that this had become his favorite spot on the river.

Perhaps the hardest sell of all were the riverside observation decks that now jut out over the river. Even Dan's architect opposed him on that one.

"I wanted to have these decks where people could sit and watch the river," he says. "They all thought it would just be a place for people to drink and smoke pot."

"I can only hope that a little of that is going on," he adds with a smile.

In fact the occupants of the first two decks we pass are single women, one reading and the other doing yoga, and the one we pass now holds teenagers who, in the midst of their make-out session, are oblivious to our canoe floating below. It's true that in one of the scenic clearings—so-called "interpretive sites" that Dan designed himself—two grizzled-looking men are passing a paper bag, but so far there have been exactly zero incidents of the crime that the residents feared.

At another unoccupied access point, Dan decides he needs to get out to do a little work. "Life is maintenance," my father told me not long before he died. It was not the sort of thing my romantic young self wanted to hear, but it is something I now at least half-acknowledge as true. Certainly it's something Dan has come to believe in his work along the river. The big vision and big victories are nice but then comes the day-to-day work of maintaining those gains, making sure the river doesn't sink back into another of its dark forgotten periods. Dan demonstrates this for me in the flesh as we land near a small path down to the water that is overgrown with weeds. At first he just wants to show me the landing but then he doesn't like the way the weeds have encroached on the path and the way someone has left a soda can under the brush and, before he knows it, it has turned into a project. Dan bursts into a flurry of activity, again employing his paddle as machete, and tearing back vines with his hands. He smashes down knotweed with his paddle while avoiding the blue flag iris.

"You just saw how I've been maintaining this same little area for five years. It takes basically about three or four minutes of crushing some knotweed and a little edgework on the boulders and you're done. The maintenance guys do a good job. But they have a hard time doing anything other than cutting grass. That's what they like to do. Cut grass."

We paddle past the Bleachery Dye Works where, less than a hundred years ago, the river's color changed almost daily with the factory's discharge: purple, red, brown, like a twisted Willy Wonka nightmare. Today, branches span over the mostly naturally colored river. An Eastern kingbird peers down from one branch. Then a floating can of Bud Light bobs by, followed, a few seconds later, by a female Baltimore oriole flying past.

"The thing is that for all the work and fighting you don't really have to do that much to heal a place," Dan says with a laugh. "You just get it started and nature does the rest."

Proof is the floodplain through which we float: a classic silver maple forest with roots that crawl over the bank like snakes. Painted turtles rest on snags and black crowned night herons roost in the trees and kingfishers shoot out over the river. It's true we have to occasionally avoid half-submerged cinderblocks and shopping carts, but if this is a limited and battered wilderness, it is also a resilient and recovering one.

As we paddle toward the city, I think back on how it all

started for Dan. Somebody at work told him to go look
at old maps of the river, giving the new kid something to
do. Dan did look at those maps. And then, over the next
seventeen years or so, he threw himself into reclaiming
the junkyards and car parks and industrial wastelands that
had sprung up along the Charles, shepherding in a green
resurgence on the riverbanks by taking back land that had
once belonged to the state but that had gradually been il-
legally encroached upon by businesses and neighbors. He
literally changed the maps. His quixotic goal was to sell
the idea of the Charles — a river made famous in song for
just how dirty it was — as a nature preserve while wran-
gling, talking, and legislating land away from encroach-
ing factory owners, homeowners, and even that local
Mafioso in his attempt to restore native plants and trees
to create a green corridor through the heart of Boston.

Dan's was an odd quest, no doubt about it, but in this
age of environmental losses and hand-wringing, perhaps the
oddest thing about it was this:

It was successful.

 FLIGHT

Waltham is the first community after eighty-one miles of Charles where the river no longer serves as a continuous border. It is a substantially poorer town, and a tougher town, than those where the Charles begins. But it is here, deep in the city, that you get a real feel for the remnant wildness of the tamed river. Even though you've got supermarkets and warehouses lurking behind, when you are actually on the river there's still a true, riparian, wild feel. There is a practical reason for this: not too many people want to portage through the center of Waltham as we did with the help of Juan and Wilson, which means we get the water to ourselves.

"This is near the confluence of Beaver Brook and the Charles. Beaver Brook leads up to Beaver Brook Reservation—the first public reservation as part of a metropolitan system in the US. It's fascinating terrain."

To think of the city as *terrain!* Territory to fight over and claim for the tribe.

Open mussel shells litter the river floor along with the occasional piece of trash. The trees aid the wildness, blocking out the city. Great silver maples span the river, their leaves a light chalky green, some of the largest trees left within the commuter circle of Route 128, preserved at first by neglect and now by law.

And of course, another thing that helps are the birds. Jays, mallards, chipping sparrows, Eastern kingbirds, and a kingfisher too. In my dry bag I have a list of the birds I've seen over the last three days and it contains more than thirty species.

"The strange thing," Dan says. "Is that you likely see more birds here, close to the city."

I ask why.

"Well, we're closing in on the harbor so you get sea-birds too. And this stretch is smack dab in the middle of the North American flyway. And because of the dams no one really paddles here. Which means it's a kind of small wildlife refuge."

I remember the jungled stretch of water we paddled yesterday and the sharp-shinned hawk we saw weaving its way through the branches. I can't help but think aloud how amazing it is for an animal to have evolved to maneuver in tight between trees and branches.

Then, thinking about Dan's story about the black crowned night herons, I remember that during the year my daughter was born, when we lived in Cambridge, I regularly got out to the river to watch herons too. His story of being renewed by the birds may sound hokey to some, but it rings true to me. My friends may give me a hard time for how much I write about birds, but the fact is that birds, more than anything else, have led to my transformation into this creature called an environmentalist. So much of my environmental life has begun with, and sprung from, birds.

I admit this to Dan.

"It makes sense," he says. "It all starts with simply look-ing around. And when you look around these days you're unlikely to see too many grizzly bears, whales, or cougars. But you can still see a lot of birds."

Birds then, oddly, considering how high they fly, are nature's lowest common denominators.

✕

We face another long portage in the middle of Watertown. Dan stays with the boats and sends me off for supplies at the local Store 24. After all this exertion, I feel I can guiltlessly eat anything, which shows in my selection: a store-heated cheesesteak, a bag of Ruffles, a Hostess blueberry pie, and assorted other junk food. Dan grunts with disgust at my offerings, and I have to admit that, as hungry as I am, it does not sit well.

We are not looking forward to carrying the canoe again. At the Store 24 I tried to call for help. One of my oldest friends, Mark Honerkamp, lives not a quarter mile from where we now sit, but he didn't pick up the phone when I called. Honerkamp's life has been ruled, over the last decade, by the cycles of the fishing season. Once April comes round he spends every weekend, and every spare moment, heading out to the Wachusetts Reservoir, an hour to the West. He keeps a notebook where he harvests count-less observations of the weather, wind, birds, and animals he sees. When he does consent to pick up his phone the news he bears is not of the worldly sort, but rather the fact that he saw river otters near the dam above the reservoir. Closer to home, Honerkamp has been one of the chief beneficiaries of Dan Driscoll's work, so that now, with a short stroll from his house, he can head to the water below Watertown Dam and see if the herring are running.

Honerkamp's beginnings as a nature-lover might have come straight out of David Sobel's mind. He grew up in different times than my daughter or any young children today. As a ten-year-old, he lived in upstate New York and his mother's passion was dog shows. The shows were usually on the weekends, and the night before the show, she and her son would find a map of the area they were visiting and look for a river. The next day they would drive to the area and, following the map, find an area where river and road ran close to one another. Son would then kiss mother goodbye and scramble down the bank with his pole and gear. He would spend the day fishing while she spent it watching dogs perform, and then, at a pre-arranged time, they would meet again on the road.

Leave aside the fact that such behavior would get his mother arrested today and focus on the fact that that time outdoors imprinted itself on the young Honerkamp. He learned, not just about the animals that swam below the water, but those that flew above it. In more recent years, he has accompanied me on many of my nature adventures, following ospreys to Venezuela for instance, and, since his eyes and ears are sharper than mine, I have come to defer to him in the matter of bird identification. But neither of us are real birders. We are rather two guys who feel our lives are lifted when we pay attention to the creatures who are flying through them. Lowest common denominator, indeed.

I began this section by talking about birds, and I'd like to end that way too.

To Nordhaus and Shellenberger this must be the worst sort of old school foolishness. Another cobwebbed Rachel Carson tale. But you've gone off-track *again*, I hear Nord and Shell saying. You're supposed to be talking about

environmentalism and saving the world, and here you
are yammering on and on about birds. Come on, give us
a break: This is just another branch of the same nut job
extremist stuff you were railing against before. Enough with
the birds!

For all you do-gooders out there, it might seem like I'm
working backwards. You are already acting environmen
tally, so what's all this about birds? Perhaps all I am really
suggesting is taking a little time to get to know the world
you are working so hard to save. If you are willing to do
this, birds are not a bad way to start. Pick a bird, any bird.
Watch it for a while: note its habits, note what it eats, how
it flies. Note its priorities and how it goes about being in
the world, based on those priorities, in a manner different, but similar, to human beings. Keep it up and after a
while you might find your brain migrating outward. I'm
not saying that you will find yourself flying out of self, like
Wordsworth or Emerson or something. But you might feel
the first tugging of outward movement, the beginning of
something. (Notice I said go look at a bird. I didn't say go
bird-watching or bird-cataloguing or bird identifying.)

"It all starts by looking around," Dan said. I like that.
But why is looking so important? Because looking outward,
noticing someone, or something, is usually the first step toward falling in love. How does love start after all? As a crush,
a surface attraction that deepens with time and knowledge,
leading to a larger, longer, more consistent commitment.

You can't force love, of course, everyone tells us so, but
you can be open to it.

Often it begins by accident. My own love of ospreys
began with a walk out on a local jetty. That walk led to
several years spent observing the birds. I can honestly

say that since I discovered ospreys my life has radiated
outward from them. I realize that I am on the verge of
slipping into just the sort of gooey, lovey-dovey OSPREY-
WARBLING mysticism that I ridiculed earlier. It's hard to
talk about these transcendent emotions without sounding
silly. But from a hard-nosed, practical point of view, I have
always found that birds work quite efficiently as a means of
transport. They work well in part because they are close,
physically close, the closest many of us come to wildness.
And they work because we don't have to backpack through
Alaska to find them: they come to us, flitting through
our lives. You may find that something else triggers wildness in you — frogs, maybe, or plants, or soil — but birds
are what do it for me. Simply watching them go about
their wild business of flight. I'm somewhat easy in this
regard: really any bird that flies through my life will do.
Ospreys work but so do gannets plunging into the ocean
or pelicans soaring overhead in all their pterodactyl glory.

Black skimmers work, too. This past fall I developed a
crush on these small birds on the Southern beach where
I now live, and they may provide a concrete example of
the transport I'm talking about. It's hard not to get excited when you see these strange little creatures scything
along the shoreline. I would dare you to stay in your own
mumbling head, running around on the same hamster
wheel of thought, would dare you, as they mow the water,
scooping up tiny fish with their preposterous bills, to not
at least momentarily skip out of yourself. Of course I
know you *can* resist, know you can stay stubbornly in your
mind. Skimmers are not the only miraculous animals after
all, and human beings excel, beyond all else, at becoming absorbed in their own obsessions. But if you actually

turn away from those stories and look at these birds for
a moment, really *look*, you'll need to pause thought and
briefly rearrange the way you think about the world.

Here is what you'll see:

A line of birds flying along the shore, the size of small
gulls but unmistakably not gulls. Maybe they're terns, you
think for a second, but like no terns you've ever seen. An
electric red-orange patch shines out from the upper sheath
of their long bills and then there are the bills themselves:
candy-corn orange-red like something from the pages of a
comic book, certainly not real birds. But they are real, these,
the only birds that have a lower mandible longer than the
upper, the better for scooping. They patrol the shore, jaws
dropped (like yours maybe), grazing the water and hoping
for accidental contact with a fish. Then, if they do touch a
fish, the merest touch, a built-in tactile trigger in their jaw
sends a signal to their upper bill, the maxilla, which instanta-
neously snaps shut.

This sounds miraculous, a thing of wonder, but of
course to the fish it is a different, not so wonder-filled, story.
To the fish the skimmer's oversized lower mandible cutting
through the water might as well be the reaper's scythe. But
you won't worry too much about the fish as you watch the
bird fly belly to belly with the sea, so close that its reflec-
tion seems to fly below it through the water. Instead you'll
watch that lower mandible, the very front part, kicking
up the small wake as it plows forward. You'll notice that
the birds actually leave a line behind them in the water.

Curious, maybe, you'll learn more. You'll learn that
skimmers were once called "Sea Dogs" for the strange
garbled barking sounds they make. You'll learn that, like
us, they are creatures of edges; they thrive at dawn or dusk,

harvesting the edge of water and land, working the edges between day and night. Your field guide will wax poetic about their flight, about how they execute hairpin turns and smooth banks while foraging, how their flocks wheel in unison. The guide will also confirm what your eyes tell you: that their heads are held down below their wings and that their flight is "buoyant." As you read on, it may occur to you that evolutionists and creationists could fight for hours over this bird. Days maybe. Who, after all, the latter group would argue, but a creator, and a creator with a sense of humor, could have created *this*? The joke shop nose, the funny barking, the crazy way of getting dinner. The former group would rebut that the silly bill is fit exactly to its task, and so could have evolved into no other shape. The only thing the two camps will agree on, throwing up their hands, will be the bizarre uselessness of the candy-corn color of the bill. They will all shrug and call it beyond comprehension.

You may become greedy for skimmers. You'll start planning your walks for dawn or dusk so that you can see them gracefully mowing the water. One day, as if to further emphasize just how strange these birds are, you'll see a hundred skimmers plopped down on the sand as if they'd just decided, then and there, that they'd had it. It is a strange sight, one you've never seen before with any birds: They have all dropped themselves chest first on the sand—gone *kaput*—and stretched their bills forward as if too tired to go on. Later your field guide will reassure you that this is common skimmer behavior, not just a flock of particularly exhausted birds.

Of course skimmers will not solve any of your life's problems. To say that you will return from your walks changed is an exaggeration. Maybe you'll barely remember

the sight of the scything birds during the rest of your
busy day. Perhaps you'll never even mention them to
your spouse. But if not fundamentally changed, you are
in some unspoken way at least mildly altered. At the very
least you've experienced a blip in the day's habitual worry.
Perhaps, better yet, those sharp bills have given you a cutting gift, slicing through the nettles of thought. And perhaps
the birds have allowed those tapes in your head to stop for
a moment, long enough for you to briefly notice that there
are vast worlds beyond your own.

IV. INDEPENDENCE DAY

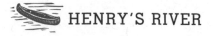 HENRY'S RIVER

When most people think of the Charles, they picture the Basin, the wide city river of boathouses and colleges and scullers, where the river briefly goes to the Ivy League. Right now that Basin is filling with boats, everyone anticipating tonight's fireworks and Pops concert, and I will be joining them, hitching a ride in a canoe with some scientists from Woods Hole and watching the fireworks up close. The reason I will need to hitch that ride is that Dan has decided to pull the canoe out just short of Harvard. He has places to be, and anyway, this stretch of river, the fancy, man-made river, isn't for him.

"They won't let me put in a natural landscape here," he grumbles, "And there's too much lawn—it becomes a festival of goose crap. They mow the grass on the banks so it's like a golf course. My goal all along has been to create a natural, varied ecosystem—a dynamic landscape. If you don't want geese then plant native plantings, not *grass*."

I ask if there are any creative possibilities for re-wilding the Basin.

"Maybe if they let me blow up Storrow Drive. Then you could make that a corridor of trees with a path down the middle. . . ."

But even to someone with Dan's environmental imagination, the possibilities near downtown are limited: Highways on both sides sandwich the Charles so that it looks like the middle of three parallel-running rivers.

"You can't replant roads," Dan admits. On the other
hand, he points out with a smile, there have been recent
winter sightings of coyote footprints on the frozen river.
We aren't the only ones who think of the river as a path.

Just above Harvard we climb out of the boat. Donna
is there to pick up Dan and our goodbye is a hurried one.
But the plan is to meet up again tonight, downtown above
the esplanade, on the rooftop of one of Dan's friends'
homes, where we can toast our trip and watch the fireworks. Dan makes sure that I don't want a ride, and I tell
him that I will either hitch a ride in one of the many boats
heading downtown, or will simply stroll along the river. In
turn I make sure he doesn't want to paddle the final few
miles with me. No, work and family obligations press.

Donna pulls him away before he can start scheming again,
and, with their canoe strapped to the roof of the car, they
rumble out of the parking lot. I have changed into my first
dry clothes in days, a rumpled Hawaiian shirt and shorts.
The riverbank is bustling with people and boats and I doubt
I'll have trouble talking my way into a ride down to the Hatch
Shell. But for now I don't mind being alone. My ideas for a
new environmentalism, my green manifesto, have mostly
been confined to a small boat, and I want to air them out. I've
stretched Dan and his story just about as far as I can, and as I
stroll east up the river and cut up Mount Auburn to Harvard
Square, it is another Massachusetts boy, born only twenty miles
or so from Dan's hometown, who begins to occupy my mind.

When I first began thinking seriously about my "green
manifesto," I scribbled these words:

Now dressed in full nature writing regalia — spear
in hand and animal pelts on — I am finally ready to

do battle. I am ready to leave behind the effete fear
that politics will somehow taint my work, to understand that this exclusion is mere fashion, and that
fashions change. I am also ready to leave behind the
nature writer's sense of impotence. What I want to
carry into the fight is humor, irony, and the personal
essayist's recourse to the testing ground of self.
What I want to leave behind is "Oh, how lovely!"
while what I want to carry into the fight are the
moments — often lovely moments, yes — when I am
briefly outside of myself, moments that remind me
of how multifarious and delightful this world still
is and that speak to my own animal wildness. What
I want to leave behind is false romanticism. What I
want to carry into the fight is the original romantic
urge for the specific, the local, the real. What I want
to leave behind is quoting Thoreau; what I want
instead is to follow more deeply the complex spirit
of the man. What I want to leave behind are pages
of facts. What I want to carry forward are facts
marshaled for purpose, facts enlivened because they
follow an idea. What I want to leave behind is the
sanctimony of quietude and order and "being in the
present." What I want to embrace is loud and wild
disorder, growing this way and that, lush and overdone. What I want to leave behind is the virtuous
and the good, and move toward the inspiring and
great. And while we're at it I want to leave behind
anything false, false to me that is, false to what I
feel is my experience on this earth. What I want
instead is to wade through the mess of life without
ever reaching for a life ring called The Answer.

My dream is to fight and to rally others to my
fight. And here is my cry:

Nature writers of the world unite. You have nothing to lose but your daisy chains.

I've tried to stick to some of these vows, but in at
least one way I've failed miserably. It turns out I can't quit
Thoreau. While vowing to stop quoting him was easy,
actually stopping has been close to impossible. Either it
is because I am a kind of Thoreau addict, or because the
man keeps pointing back to what I see as the true root
of living a wild life. Here in Cambridge, for instance, I
can't help but include these thoughts of Henry's about
the section of river I am now walking, thoughts that he
scribbled down on a July night 156 years before my stroll:

Coming out of town — willingly as usual, — when
I saw that reach of Charles River just above the
depot, the fair, still water this cloudy evening suggesting the way to eternal peace and beauty, whence
it flows, the placid lake-like fresh water, so unlike
the salt brine, affected me not a little. I was reminded of the way in which Wordsworth so coldly
speaks of some natural visions or scenes "giving
him pleasure." This is perhaps the first vision of
Elysium on this route from Boston. And just then
I saw an encampment of Penobscots, their wig-
wams appearing above the railroad fence, they, too,
looking up the river as they sat on the ground, and
enjoying the scene. What can be more impressive
than to look up a noble river just at evening — one,
perchance, which you have never explored — and

behold its placid waters, reflecting the woods and
sky, lapsing inaudibly toward the ocean; to behold
a lake, but know it as a river, tempting the beholder
to explore it and his own destiny at once? Haunt of
waterfowl. This was above the factories—all that
I saw. That water could never have flowed under a
factory. How *then* could it have reflected the sky?

Maybe the reason it's hard to stop quoting him is that
he seems to have been every place I go. Hell, he even
wrote his own book about going down a river with a
buddy, his brother, and that river, like mine, had its source
in Hopkinton. Furthermore it was on this very same day
of the year—July Fourth—that Thoreau moved into his
cabin on Walden Pond just a short 156 years ago.

But I am not a complete Thoreau groupie. We have
our differences. As I cut across Mass Ave into Harvard
Square, I remember that Thoreau, a thoroughly me-
diocre student, saw Harvard as a kind of prison, or at
least half-way house, before he could head back to the
wilds of Concord. For me, my brief stint as a lecturer
in environmental writing here six years ago was one
of the wildest times of my life. It wasn't just the birth
of my daughter, which served as a joyous confirma-
tion of my suspicion that we are all animals. It was that
I saw my time in the city as a kind of challenge. If I
could find wildness here then I could find it anywhere.

And I did find it, in the red-tailed hawks that hunted near
the Johnson Gate and the straw and sticks of swallows' nests
that spilled out of the gargoyle lions' mouths and every
other architectural crevice and in the coyotes that I tracked
through Boston's suburbs. I don't know that I have had a

time when I ever felt quite so alive, though I suspect this had more than a little to do with the fact that my daughter was drawing her first breaths.

She was born May seventh and Harvard Yard during those May days spilled over. As the buds on the fruit trees burgeoned, thoughts of birth, of potential, of early blooming exploded in my mind. I read up on the history of the place, too, and discovered that, in 1837, the year Thoreau graduated from Harvard, Ralph Waldo Emerson delivered the school's Phi Beta Kappa address. For the occasion he composed a little essay called "The American Scholar" in which he wrote:

> Men, such as they are, very naturally seek money or power; and power because it is as good as money, — the 'spoils,' so called, 'of office.' And why not? For they aspire to the highest, and this, in their sleep-walking, they dream is the highest. Wake them and they shall quit the false good and leap to the true, and leave governments to clerks and desks.[21]

No one knows if Thoreau, as a graduating senior, actually heard those words spoken, but there is no doubt he read them soon after. Imagine what that was like. Talk about lighting a fuse for a bomb. Talk about setting a young mind on fire.

What we forget in these cynical days is that the same fuse can still be lit. We are so convinced that this sort of idealism is a mere historical relic. But I am not so sure. "Nothing is diminished," wrote the poet A.R. Ammons. Okay, sure, yes, much is really diminished. The world is doomed, the world is crowded, we are up shit's creek. But still, *nothing is diminished*. Every year the buds on these fruit trees fill, bulge, and burst. The birds fly over, the world waits.

✕

Let's clear away the bullshit and cut to the chase.

Let's get down to a simple question, a question befitting an address to graduating seniors. Here it is: *What is the meaning of life?*

Let's start with one of Thoreau's answers. It's fairly straightforward: fall in love with the world. But how does this translate into practical action? Maybe through the oldest form of recreation, older even than jet skiing or poker. And what is that mysterious activity? I'm afraid my answer can't help but be anti-climactic: it is the activity I am engaged in at this very moment. Walking.

I'm sorry, but isn't that where it starts? With apologies to the yogis who are reading this, most of us don't have a taste for sitting still. We think better in movement, and in concert with the world. Wandering off for no apparent reason may not have the environmental zing of low carbon cars but it too serves a purpose, even if that purpose sometimes seems purposeless. First of all, it's the best way to see the world. For us bipedal creatures, it has always been. It's how we got from Africa to here. And I'm convinced that for most of us, it's when we think best, with our feet connected to the ground. Thoreau said of going for a walk: "If you are ready to leave father and mother, and brother and sister, and wife and child and friends, and never see them again—if you have paid your debts, and made your will, and settled all your affairs, and are a free man, then you are ready for a walk."[22]

What the hell does that mean? It means that we spend

the better part of our lives trying to be logical, trying to be practical, trying to follow through on our commitments and checking things off our lists, but that sometimes, maybe once a day, we need to launch ourselves out the door and head to a place, both physical and mental, that we can call our own. Granted, that is a bit hard in a world with six billion people, but it still can be done. I live on a crowded beach that serves as the town's promenade, but can still manage to find cracks in the day when I have it almost to myself. True, I grumble at the other people I run into who dare walk *my* beach, but more often I reach a feeling of being out on my own. And what does that get me? Well, practically speaking, nothing.

I don't want to wander too far down the Luddite road of my eco-brethren but I do need to suggest that the kind of walking I am talking about is best done devoid of cell phones and iPods. Yes, I know that this leads toward what is possibly the most terrifying of human paths: the one to boredom. But once we sink down below this uneasy sensation we may find that the world is distraction enough. Waves turn out to actually be kind of interesting. Pelicans, too. And watching northern gannets dive, well forget about it.

It's a great show—like some kind of hybrid of opera and ultimate fighting—full of contact and joy and immersion. A powerful bird dives down from the sky headfirst, and spears into the water, and then a hundred of its kind do the same, a dozen striking in a second.

I suspect that ninety-nine percent of the people who walk the same beach never see this drama. This does not make them bad people. But if they took a break from their self-arguments and preconceptions, and simply stared out at the water for a minute or two, they might notice that there, out beyond the waves, is something even more dramatic than any popular distraction. They might experience a kind of wild delight as the birds plunge recklessly into the water.

And so what? So nothing. So nothing practical maybe. But perhaps — and I admit this may be overreaching — perhaps the beginning of something, the stirring of sympathy with the world. And perhaps a moment when, however fleetingly, they step out of their own lives and into the lives of the birds.

So walking, too, is part of my larger platform as I create my green manifesto. A good walk leads you to places you don't expect. Most often, however, a good walk also circles back home. In our case, it brings us back to the idea of fighting for the world. It reminds us that we are not just fighting for an energy policy or parklands — though we are certainly fighting for those things too — but that what we are really fighting for is something irrational, something ineffable, something at odds with what most of us consider goals and ideals. The good news is that that something is still out there and that it is wild and that wildness is always changing. The good news is that, as a bonus, to fight for this nameless thing is fulfilling. The good news is that fighting for it — in one's own way, a way one finds the way a writer finds a voice — is not a bad way to spend your time on Earth.

But it can't be that simple. Walking can't be the answer to life's primary question . . . Freud's answer was Love and Work. Donald Hall, in his wonderful book, *Life Work*, suggests that the secret to life is absorption. To be fully absorbed in something. To find something you do well and throw your whole self into it. Even typing those words I get excited. To have a great and exciting project. One's

first instinct might be that the project should be manage-
able, small, achievable. But it turns out that, the way most
of our minds work, it's even better if the project is massive, deep, unachievable. It turns out that many of us like
our challenges steep, and that it is steepness — even near-
impossibility — that engages our imaginations in unexpected ways. When we last left Dan Driscoll on the Charles
he was not merely "being in the present moment," though
he was certainly enjoying floating down the river, but was
dreaming and scheming about what he would do next. And
why not? Tell me to pick up one soda can and I may sulk,
but suggest I clean the whole city and there's a chance I
will become *engaged*.

A few pages back I vowed not to quote Thoreau, to put
him aside. It's a vow I haven't stuck to very well, and now
I'd like to abandon it entirely. What does Thoreau offer in
way of answer to our big question? For one thing Henry
David Thoreau, I contend, was a workaholic. The fact that
he walked in the woods for four hours each day, or that he
loafed by the pond doesn't undermine but supports my
thesis, since, I would argue, those activities were part of
his job description. Most of us aren't actually very good
at loafing; our brains won't have it. We stay still, but our
minds don't. They fly this way and that, hungry, searching,
never quite satisfied. What are they looking for? I'll suggest
that one answer might be an all-consuming project. That's
certainly what Thoreau had in Concord. A love affair with
his hometown, but also a great project, a mission, to know
that place as deeply as he could, to walk it and learn it and
survey it and record it and talk it and smell it and really truly
know it. The fruits of this project weren't just *Walden* or his
journals, but the fact that his observations of the phenology

of his place — the return of birds, the flowering of the plants, for instance — were accurate enough to still be used by scientists today to plot the changes that global warming has wrought. The old cliché about Thoreau was that he grew dry and uninspired in his last years, that he forsook his early romantic ardor for more clinical observations of the succession of trees and other scientific matters, but that was just a part of his larger project, too, his job description changing slightly, and I think the project would have carried on for many, many years had he not died young.

Thoreau is also often portrayed as the prophet of sacrifice, of "doing without." Yes, he sacrificed and simplified, but he did it in service to his larger project, and that makes all the difference. Too often environmentalism gets tarred with the same brush: it is seen as a philosophy of renunciation, of living a drab dull life. But sacrifice toward creating something larger isn't dull, it's exciting. Mere renunciation, on the other hand, mere doing without, has got about the same chance of success, and the same appeal, as the Pope's abstinence argument. In fact, the great flaw of the abstinence argument is the flaw of many environmental arguments: asking humans to be something they are not. Of course there has to be some sacrifice but the sacrifice has to be in service of something, some idea of where we are headed. And it would help greatly if that idea were *exciting*.

Excitement is a concept that some environmentalists are quite down on, associated as it is with so-called unnatural diversions like video games and porn. But excitement also means a life of goals and energy, of disputes and vows, of dreaming and scheming, of competition and revenge, of magnanimity. I'd like an environmentalism that embraces that kind of life, not one that is always seeking to convert us all into St. Francis of Assisi. An environmentalism that insists we be something other than what we are, something new-and-improved, something beyond human, will not succeed. But an environmentalism that draws on what we are has a much better shot.

Remember Henry Moore's reply when Donald Hall asked him what the meaning of life was: "It needs to be something that you spend your whole life trying to do but can't possibly achieve." It is true that the stock market might provide deep immersion for some, and crossword puzzles for others. But what Thoreau discovered with his project was that there is nothing more exciting than having the outside world as the object of your affection. Why not have a love affair with the world itself? Everyone likes to quote Thoreau and he gets pulled in a hundred different directions by a hundred different groups until he finally looks like the scarecrow after the flying monkeys got hold of him, his stuffing pulled out. But those who try to make him into a purely political figure forget what a small part of his life that was. The political element, the small moments of activism, were mere outgrowths of the larger project of both immersing himself in the world and creating a self. Salvation, Thoreau taught, begins at home. Yes, his night in jail inspired Gandhi and Martin Luther King, but here was a man whose great passionate project was the individual self, living as well and honestly and nakedly as he could, and who found a match for that self in the physical world, the world of animals and trees and water and plants. And as it turned out his discovery of the world was what unlocked a greater self. As it turned out the world was exciting enough to make the sacrifices worth it. As it turned out the world wasn't just interesting but *thrilling*.

HEY, HEY WE'RE THE MONKEYS

Dan Driscoll has little use for Harvard. The school,
and the others like MIT and B.U. that like to feature the
Charles on their brochure covers, don't have a lot of interest in returning a varied ecosystem to the river.

"They reap the benefits of a revitalized river but you
can't get a cent out of them," he said not long before
he climbed out of the canoe. "You'd think they'd want
to spend a little of that zillion dollar endowment. Not
a chance."

When Dan was invited to speak at the school, he found
that it only brought out the contrarian in him. He repeated
for his learned crowd what he had said to me on our first
day on the river:

"Real environmental awareness may not be possible
without hallucinogens," he told them.

Maybe the audience laughed; maybe they thought him
silly. Dan claimed not to care.

"I believe in anything that turns us away from the
virtual world to the real one," he said.

I understand Dan's antipathy toward Harvard. But
during my single term teaching here, between births and
coyotes and birds and happily engaged students, I can't say
I share Dan's assessment.

I walk up to Adams House, where I wheeled Hadley
over the cobblestones during her first weeks, loudly lulling
her to sleep. Sean Palfrey, who is Teddy Roosevelt's great

grandson, was the Adams House "master" when we were
there, and he showed me the crib the young TR was rocked
in. Hadley's was a rare, poetic beginning, as we were rent-
ing a room that was usually occupied by the poet Seamus
Heaney. "All children want to crouch in their secret nests,"
Heaney once wrote. We found the poet's things-to-do lists
and notes on how to program the VCR and took them as
a blessing.

It was during that luscious spring that I became, for the
first time, a teacher as well as a father. In the years since I
have become the sort of animal known as a professor, but
from the beginning I vowed that I would bring wildness into
the classroom. I brought in coyote skulls and bird feathers,
and tried to keep in mind that most of the time when I was
a student I'd been bored to death, and to remember just how
dead the assigned reading often felt to me. Early on I learned
that one good way to break students out of the deadly apathy
of the classroom is to literally break them out. Taking classes
outdoors, really outdoors, does wonders, and I've made it a
staple of my teaching for years. It's amazing how much more
animated grad students become about books, for instance,
when they discuss them after a couple of drinks around a
bonfire, after kayaking out to a deserted island where they will
spend the night in a tent. I can't legally recommend skinny
dipping at midnight with those same students as a pedagogical
tool, but, theoretically at least, it is not ineffective. The point
is to get outside, to engage, to make some kind of contact.

Last fall I taught a class of both grad students and
undergrads called "When Thoreau Met Darwin." The
two men may seem strange bedfellows at first, but there
is more overlap than you might think. Of course Thoreau
and Darwin never actually met, but their great books,

Walden and *The Origin of Species*, were published within
three years of each other, in 1856 and 1859, respectively.
And while it is unlikely that Darwin ever read a sentence
of *Walden*, Thoreau read *The Voyage of the Beagle* with
keen interest. Then in 1860, two years before he died at
forty-four, Thoreau got his hands on Darwin's *Origin*.

Many once believed that Thoreau's last years were
wooden ones, his transcendental fervor having died out.
Thankfully Robert D. Richardson, the author of *Henry
Thoreau: A Life of the Mind*, came along to overturn this mis-
interpretation. In fact, reading Darwin sparked Thoreau to a
massive study of the leafing of Concord's trees and the blos-
soming and fruiting of plants, a comprehensive phenological
chronicling of his hometown that promised a new beginning
in Thoreau's writing, a movement away from the more personal focus of *Walden* and toward a wider, biocentric view
of nature. It was a movement that mirrored Darwin's ideas,
ideas that transformed *Homo sapiens* from the central role in
the world's drama into just another player.

One of the real pleasures of reading the two men at
once was the way that both of their minds wandered
freely over disciplines. For instance, Darwin, as well as
studying ornithology, geography, history, and a dozen
other fields, was also a hell of a writer—amiable, straightforward, and as clear as he could be given that he was trying
to explain something fairly technical and entirely new.
It doesn't hurt that when he needs to he can draw on his
seven year study of barnacles and drop a mean crustacean
reference. Or that he can reference fantails or short-faced
tumblers or pouters from his decades-long study of pigeons.

Like Darwin, Thoreau was immensely curious.
Richardson writes of Thoreau's inspired reaction to reading

Origin: "That his interests were still expanding, his wonder still green, his capacity for observation, expression, and connection still growing is the most impressive evidence that his spirits this January were still on the wing."[23] But while Thoreau wrote constantly, he shied away from the professionalism that the title of writer implied. Writing was part of a larger project called living. "The head is an organ for burrowing," he writes. His was a lifelong experiment in burrowing, working his way down through the "mud and slush of opinion, and prejudice, and tradition, and delusion, and appearance, that allusion which covers the globe."[24] For his part, Darwin was perhaps history's greatest *connector*, his interests extending from barnacles to pigeons to how "the presence of feline animals in large numbers in a district might determine, through the intervention first of mice and then of bees, the frequency of certain flowers in that district!"[25] For many years Darwin was, like Thoreau, a reporter to "a journal, of no very wide circulation."[26] This last quote is Thoreau's punning reference to the fact that he was the only one who read most of what he wrote. And while Thoreau had his journals to report to, Darwin had his private notebooks, which for twenty years kept the secret of natural selection to themselves while the world waited. It is there he pieced together the great puzzle, a puzzle that would forever change how human beings thought of themselves.

The students in the class were very sharp and you could see the electricity in the air as they made unexpected connections between science and literature. While they had to labor their way through *Walden*, you could watch the impact that Thoreau made, particularly with his pronouncements of nonconformity, about living a life different (and perhaps better!) than the life expected of them. Yes, you could almost see the kids thinking, there are other choices, other ways. As much as I liked my grad students, it was the undergrads who were the real pleasure, watching them come to terms with what these strange ideas might mean for their lives.

I don't want to stretch the term "wildness," to make its meaning too elastic, but certainly one of the things they were thinking about was how they might live a wilder life—a life less predictable, less standard issue, less like the life they were expected to live. Would they end up going through with it? Who knew? But at least it was a possibility, part of the equation, and at least some new ideas were at play in their minds. That was enough. One night we gathered around one of those bonfires out on a nearby island and I was amazed, and impressed, when, rather than devolving to topics like sports or the latest party, the students kept talking late into the night about Darwin and Thoreau.

One thing the students kept mentioning, and one thing that wound its way like a stream through everything we talked about in the class, was that both books, in their different ways, reinforced the fact that human beings are part of the animal kingdom. *You are an Animal* might as well have been the course's subtitle. At least that was what everything we read during the term seemed to shout at us. And what good does it do to admit to this wildness, this animality? Well, maybe it doesn't do much good but maybe there's this: Maybe it's healthy to have our definitions come in line with our reality. And maybe there is another reason that understanding that we are animals is vital. Maybe we need to keep reminding ourselves that, as John Hay said, we are still part of this world.

Reading Thoreau and Darwin back to back certainly

helps reinforce this fact. Obviously Darwin's way of reminding us of our animal natures is more overt, if more polite.
*Um, excuse me. Did you notice this little remnant of a tail we all
have, and how it just so happens that these bones suggest that we
might have common ancestors?* Stephen Jay Gould, in the first
essay of his first collection, *Ever Since Darwin*, quotes what
he calls a "remarkable epigram" from one of Darwin's notebooks: "Plato says in *Phaedo* that our 'imaginary ideas' arise
from the preexistence of the soul, and are not derivable
from experience — read monkeys for preexistence."[27] Read
monkeys! Of course Darwin was never so direct in his great
book, only hinting that this whole evolution thing might actually apply to humans. "Light will be thrown on the origin
of man and his history" is about as far as he would go.[28]

Thoreau, with little patience for evidence early in his
career, was more brash. He points to the effluvia of what
we call society and shows how we, by considering ourselves above the natural world, have diluted and perverted
our natural strengths. As an essayist, Thoreau begins with
Montaigne's central assertion of humility that we are "just
another animal" and that, even on the highest throne in
the world we are still sitting on our asses.[29] He reminds
us that, at core, our main challenges on Earth remain the
getting of food and fuel and fire, something many of us are
now remembering again as such things become scarce.

What does it really mean to say, through science or art,
that we are just another animal? Different things to different
people. Some see it as sacrilege, others as a way to justify
our aggressive or territorial impulses. Maybe a better use
of this information is in moving toward a greater humility,
and an ability to see beyond our own merely anthropo-
centric needs. Maybe this can lead to not taking ourselves

quite so seriously. After all, DNA puts the lie to our myth of specialness. If it is trite to say that we are brothers and sisters with other members of the animal world, all united, then it is also simply and biologically true. But an acceptance of our own animal nature is just a starting place, and from that *base* base we can build upward. Our reaction needn't be, "Hey, we're animals, don't expect much of us." For along with humility, we can also feel some deserved confidence, since the animals we happen to be have developed not just enormous brains and opposable thumbs and complex languages, but an inherent and dazzling ability to be flexible, to adapt almost from minute to minute. Gould goes so far as to crown flexibility our defining trait, saying that it "may be the most important determinant of human consciousness."[30] We change therefore we are.

What thrills me here is the yolking of the base to the sublime, the animal to the intellectual. It's easy for our thinking to grow thin and brittle when we philosophize, to forget that we are creatures who shit and fuck and die. On the other hand, as animals we are capable of doing things like developing theories of evolution and writing books about going to live in the woods. For me the acknowledgment that we are just another animal is no less than the foundation of what it means to be human. Some may see this idea as a celebration of the anti-rational, but I don't think this is so. It is *reasonable* to understand that we are not rational, to understand that instinct, emotion, and dreams drive us, and I would argue that this acknowledgment of what we are, far from being anti-rational, can lead to a much greater reasonableness. It is when we make false claims to rationality, when we stuff down that which is deemed irrational, that things start to go haywire.

Montaigne wrote that "supercelestial thoughts lead to "subterranean conduct."[31] It is the reasonable human being who acknowledges that a streak of unreason is part of what makes us who we are.

Some might say this is a reductionist view of man that stamps out spirit and hope and beauty. I don't think so. Evolution does not deny the miracle. Evolution *is* the miracle.

Let's say for a minute that we actually take this notion that we are animals seriously. Let's say that we don't just pay it lip service, but follow through and ask: If we are animals how might we live well as animals? Be a "good animal" Emerson said. But Ralph didn't leave an instruction manual. How exactly do good animals live?

I would suggest that one thing a good animal might do is explore his or her territory. Explore it, prowl it, walk it, swim it, smell it, and even occasionally mark it. Get to know it at night, in all seasons and in all weathers. As we consider this question more deeply, it's worth looking again at what Wendell Berry called his "governing ambition." He writes:

> That summer I began to see, however dimly, that one of my ambitions, perhaps my governing ambition, was to belong fully to this place, to belong as the thrushes and the herons and the muskrats belonged, to be altogether at home here. That is still my ambition. But now I have come to see that it proposes an enormous labor. It is a spiritual ambition, like goodness. The wild creatures belong to

the place by nature, but as man I can belong to it
only by understanding and by virtue. It is an ambition I cannot hope to succeed in wholly, but I have
come to believe it is the most worthy of all.[32]

Berry is discussing his river home in Kentucky, and
perhaps the tone here is a little ministerial, even grand, given
our current theme of a *limited* wild. But let's take what
Berry says seriously for a minute. How would we act if
we were to really go along with Berry and make belonging to our homes our governing ambition? Well, first we
might think about where to live, considering, as much as
it is practical, how we could live near places and creatures,
including humans, who we actually care about, or might
grow to care about through "labor." Then, once we have
selected our place — our *territory* let's call it — we would
think about how we will choose to inhabit that place.

Thoreau answered this question by moving to Walden
and then setting up a daily regimen that consisted of four
hours of walking in the woods. Of course not all of us
have a pond to go live at for free (squatting on Emerson's
land) or an ancestral family home to return to like Berry's,
and the effect of these grand visionaries, and their grand
actions, may be to make us run away and hide, or at least
to claim, defensively, that what they did has no bearing on
us, or on the "real world." After all, when we get done with
work, with playing with our kids, with eating and drinking and sleeping, most of us don't have a four hour chunk
of time left over for frolicking with the muskrats. But, I
would argue, if we return to the idea of a limited wild,
and take what these thinkers say seriously, but also with
a small grain of salt, we might find that there are cracks

in the day, limited times when that limited wild can sneak in. And I would suggest that it is possible and even crucial to regard the place where you live, be it urban or rural, as your first wilderness, and as such more immediately vital and relevant than the national park you drive or fly to.

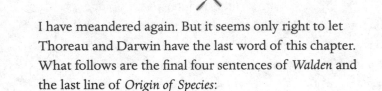

I have meandered again. But it seems only right to let Thoreau and Darwin have the last word of this chapter. What follows are the final four sentences of *Walden* and the last line of *Origin of Species*:

> The light which puts out our eyes is darkness to us. Only that day dawns to which we are awake. There is more day to dawn. The sun is but a morning star.[33]

> There is grandeur in this view of life, with its several powers having been originally breathed into a few forms or into one; and that, whilst this planet has gone cycling on according to the fixed laws of gravity, from so simple a beginning endless forms most beautiful and most wonderful have been, and are being, evolved.[34]

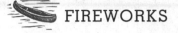 FIREWORKS

Back to my walk back down Harvard Square to the river.
It's a walk I took a hundred times during the months I
waited for my wife to give birth. For the record, Dan isn't
the only one who found something in the sight of hundreds
of night herons roosting along the Charles. And he isn't the
only one who took some solace in daily trips to the river.

In fact, it got to the point where my wife started teasing
me about it.

"Your beloved Charles," she called it.

Soon I am back on that beloved river. Cambridge is a
strange town, in many ways more complex than its cliché
image as the People's Republic of Cambridge. Yes, it is
crammed with PhDs, and is the home of Harvard and
MIT, but it is also the most racially (and internationally)
diverse of Boston's cities, and despite the gaudy prices of
Brattle Street real estate, it actually has a median household
income closer to Waltham's than Wellesley's. As I figured,
it is not too hard to bum a ride, what with everyone heading downtown to see the fireworks, and, for the small price
of the six pack of Harpoon IPA, I am now riding in luxury,
barely lifting my arm to paddle, carried forward like an
emperor in the canoe's middle.

I float the last section of the Charles in a canoe with
some MIT grads. It has been my experience that writing a book is sometimes a bit like being a healthy schizo-
phrenic, that when it's going good every person you meet,

or book you read, seems to fit perfectly into your larger
symbolic world. True to this, the woman paddling next
to us, in a small, handmade wooden kayak, turns out to
be engaged in an environmental battle of her own. Her
name is Sandy and she is an MIT scientist, and for years
she has been working to help clean up the outfall pipe, a
controversial experiment in treating Boston's sewage and
dumping it in the sea. She is fascinating and I nod from my
canoe, but what I am really thinking is that I need to take
a leak. I eye a patch of willows, which seems to me the last
private spot before the esplanade. Meanwhile the whole
town seems to have emptied out onto the streets. Hordes
head down to the Hatch Shell to watch the fireworks.

While the women in my canoe sip cherry beer home
brew, I give up all pretense of helping and put down my
paddle. Lindsay, the girl in the back, is talking nervously,
using words that are rarely found outside of the SATs, but
I am focused on the view. This section of river inspires a
regional chauvinism in me. I stare up at the MIT bridge and
then down at the Prudential and Hancock buildings. Then
there's the Citgo sign above Fenway which says Boston to
me almost as much as the next sight I see: a car being towed.

The section we are paddling was once a tidal river
and the banks where people walk were marshland. The
river was dammed and the marshes filled in, which makes
this section of the Charles about as "natural" as a ride at
Riverworld. But, having spent some pages extolling Dan
Driscoll's work to alter the river, I can hardly flip hats and
come out against this artificial section of the Charles. The
Basin is often said to serve the same purpose of Central
Park in New York, and during my own years in Boston
I took solace in getting out here whenever I could. But

compared to the section I just paddled with Dan it feels like
a city park, which is what it is after all. It may be the lack
of trees, or just the crowds both on and off the water, but I
suddenly feel ready to quit the river. My canoe hosts kindly
deposit me by the willows where, after making use of the
natural facilities, I walk the final half-mile downtown.

Storrow Drive is shut down to cars, just like in Dan's fan-
tasies. "Too bad it's not permanent," he'll say later. Yellow-
slickered state police try to keep some order but it is useless.
There are hotdogs and tents and cranes and cops and people
in biking hats and boats tied up and, by the way, over four
hundred thousand people. Powerboats fly up the river and
helicopters buzz overhead. There's still an hour before I'm
supposed to meet Dan again. I buy a hotdog and find a
spot by the river to sit that is, if not quiet, at least private,
tucked behind some bushes. From my pocket I pull the wet,
rumpled notes that I have been working on during the trip.

It occurs to me that, after spending the last few days
squabbling with Nordhaus and Shellenberger, I am ready
to reach a sort of truce. The two men do have something
important to offer to the picture of a "new environmentalist" that has been emerging from my notes. While at first I
didn't like their idea of environmentalists as "chipper entrepreneurs," I am starting to see that, if you strike the word
"chipper," there is something to this notion.

In the end I'm willing to give an inch. My definition of
this "new environmentalism" is wide, and since it is wide
it can accommodate the new entrepreneurial model, albeit
an entrepreneurial model that is rooted in the wildness of
given places we inhabit. This expanding picture fits my idea
of a less pure, less clean environmentalism. And it fits my
picture of human nature. After all, Dan Driscoll's vision

isn't a simple one. It's not a passive one either. He decided
to use his energy, his ambition, his goals, his know-how, his
persuasive abilities, everything he had to make this vision
come to pass.

What is Dan Driscoll if not an entrepreneur? Though
fired by idealism, my theoretical eco-being is essentially
pragmatic: he or she will wing a deal to save *some* land, even
if it means giving something up. That is because actually
getting something done in the world always trumps theory.
The fact is I like this picture of the new environmentalist —
eco-fighter as hustler — that is emerging. Not some guy
wearing a bearskin and speaking in hushed tones but
someone common-sensical, smart, hard-headed. Someone
who understands that for most of us the wild we fight for is
a limited wild and that we fight it with an imperfect, limited
environmentalism. This new picture is that of a man or
woman who knows how to get things done, who understands the value of momentum, of focus on a particular
project. Not a shrill or dry or particularly flowery environmentalism or environmentalist. Someone willing to get
in a fight and "Sue the bastards." Someone willing to stick
their nose in there and feel what it's like to get bruised. And
someone willing to stay locked in that fight for years, even
if it costs them emotional as well as actual capital. I remember walking through the woods as a teenager and ripping
up a dollar bill, fancying myself a new Thoreau. It's time to
store that romantic model in mothballs and remember that
the real Thoreau, as the writer Robert Sullivan has recently
pointed out, was at least in part a hard-headed entrepreneur working at innovation in the family pencil business.

Finally my fantasy eco-fighter would have a virtue that
has fallen out of favor in recent times even, and perhaps

especially, amongst environmentalists—a virtue that
Emerson and Thoreau once held in high esteem: nonconformity. I suppose you could say that what is required
is a way of looking at the world somewhat at odds with
the way that most people look at it. In fact, it may be that
an underrated aspect of committing to nature is the willingness to be considered strange. Or, at the very least,
unconventional. To be a true environmentalist is, even
within the current vogue, often to invite social ridicule.
Go ask someone not to toss their cigarette on the beach
and see what happens. Some bravery is required. There is
a possibility of conflict. Nonconformity, as necessary as it
is to accomplish new things, isn't easy. Seeking approval
is encoded in most of us, a basic component of being a
social primate. What could be easier and more natural,
and sensible, than to please the parents, to become the
doctor or lawyer or whatever? There's got to be something wrong in the kid who doesn't, something a bit off.

Even in a time when environmentalism is all the
rage, to do something truly environmental—even something as simple as asking someone to pick up litter or a
cigarette—is to invite some degree of scorn and ridicule.
So what? Scorn and ridicule are not so bad in the face
of love. When you're energized and motivated by joy
for something rather than just being *against* something,
asking someone to clean something up or think twice
doesn't feel superior or moralistic, it just feels logical.

I scribble down my emerging picture of this creation,
this prototype, my new environmentalist. Eastern but
Western. Romantic but practical. Able to quote a poem
and swing a deal. Equally unafraid of thought and action. Of course there is no such animal, or no such exact

animal. But the encouraging thing is that there are thousands of like animals, all prowling and defending their territories, all around this country and the world.

As I write, I am aware that the examples of fighters that I have used, from Dan Driscoll to Art Cooley to Ken Sleight, have their limits. Many are male, which is certainly not to say that even a majority of "fighters" are male—look at Rachel Carson, Terry Tempest Williams, Diane Wilson—just that a few of the ones that I've bumped into are. They also may tend to be a tad on the aggressive side, and are not exactly teetotalers, which again likely reflects the character of the writer who sought them out. But the beauty of the fight, and the fighters, is that they are in no way restricted to this small group or to the narrow characteristics of that group. The fact is that this ideal environmentalist does not have to be a chipper entrepreneur or even an entrepreneur at all, doesn't have to hew to any of the specific characteristics I have outlined. All they need to do is pick a fight worth fighting and then, in accordance with their own temperament, personality, and DNA, fight that fight in their own way.

$$\times$$

We couldn't have asked for better seats at the spectacle of exploding colors. I tell Dan that I like to think that the hundreds of thousands of people below are all here to celebrate the anniversary of Thoreau's move to Walden. He thinks perhaps not. Whatever the case, the now-darkened skies fill with fire and music. We are on the thirteenth floor of an apartment building at 260 Beacon Street, almost directly above the Hatch Shell, and Dan and I toast the success of our trip with the champagne our host just poured us.

Everyone goes inside when it starts to drizzle, but Dan
and I stay out, and are rewarded for our perseverance by
the roar of two planes, F-17s, that fly like fighter jets out
of *Star Wars* right at our balcony, seeming to head directly
at us before swerving away. We toast to that too. Even
two hardened nature boys can't help but be impressed.

The rain picks up but we stay outside. We've been wet
all week anyway and this is too good to miss. Boston is laid
out below us. I tell Dan about the notes I was taking earlier,
about my ideas about environmentalism, and pretty soon
he is off and running, once again preaching to my choir.

He points down below us.

"Look at Storrow Drive. Right now Boston is spending millions for this party. They spent fourteen billion
fucking dollars on the Big Dig. But try to get them
to spend a million on bike paths and re-planting and
all the sudden everyone's wailing about 'waste.'"

He shakes his head.

"One of the hardest things now is to be connected to
the land and to be working in environmental fields with
people who aren't. At my lectures I ask people if anyone
has spent time alone in nature in the last month. No one
raises their hand. That's what's missing. A lot of environmentalists are losing the sense of magic of why they
cared to begin with and just becoming these bitter rant-
ers. And if environmentalists are acting angry and beat up
and disheveled, you're not going to be something people
want to be. What people want is happiness. And if you
show that you are elated about your life and you're happy
with your life and you love it, they're going to want to
know what the formula is for that and I say the formula

206 IV. INDEPENDENCE DAY

is get out in nature. Get to the outdoors with your family. And a lot of environmentalism is so downtrodden. Oh,
we're doomed, we're fucked. People aren't drawn to it."

And what can I say to that? Nothing short of "Amen"
would seem to do. Instead I propose a toast:

"To our glorious adventure and continued wildness."

We clink our glasses and drink.

$$\times$$

But you've heard all this before. Yes, we get it, you're saying.
You and Dan are like-minded — you are a couple of kooks
who love nature and at least one of you (Dan) actually
does some good. But what does all this really have to do
with anything, and more importantly what can it do in
the face of GLOBAL WARMING? You've talked a lot and
meandered plenty, but have we really gotten anywhere?
Dan can say what he will, but the world is still doomed.
The fact that he likes to plant some plants and that you
like looking at birds and going for walks is not going to
change anything. Not really. When your daughter is your
age the world she faces will be crowded and cooked.

I will grant the cynics the fact that I don't know where the
world is heading. And I will grant them the fact that if we are
honest we need to admit that individuals acting as individuals have relatively little impact on that world. But that still
leaves the question of what to do while we are here. It is the
same question Thoreau faced, in fact it is the same question
everyone who has ever been born to this planet has faced.

If there is something egocentric about assuming we
can change the world, there is also something not unap-
pealingly human. We boomerang back to the same old

question. *What is to be done?* What can *you* and what can *I*—
individually— do right now?

These days writers of eco-manifestos are required by
law to answer that question with bullet points. I would like
to comply though I'm not sure I know how to start. It may
be my own flaw, but I still don't believe that cleaning the
lint in your drier is the surest road to changing your life. My
bullet points are, of necessity, not practical but vague and
grandiose.

I suppose it would be asking too much of this little book,
but this is my fantasy of how a reader might respond to
what I've written.

My fantasy reader would do three things.

1. Have a small love affair with something in the
   world.
2. Get in a fight.
3. Launch a larger project of self and world.

I think I've covered point number two pretty well,
how fighters begin and then continue their fights, and I'll
end on point number three. But let's circle back to the
first point, how the infatuation begins, how we fall for
the thing that we will ultimately fight to protect. Let me
begin by saying that I am not stressing "love" just because
it ultimately leads us to protect something or someone
or some place, but for its own sake. In other words, I
don't think the only thing that's worthwhile about loving a place is that it turns us into fighters, i.e. it is good
because it makes us fight. No, love is good in of itself and
that is true even if steps two and three don't follow. At first

our love has nothing to do with its usefulness, and in fact should be celebrated precisely *because* of its uselessness.

There are parallels between this sort of love and the wild places that are its object. In his famous "Wilderness Letter," Wallace Stegner spoke of the spiritual resources of wilderness beyond any obvious *uses* for recreation or extraction or development. Stegner wrote of this wilderness ideal: "Being an intangible and spiritual resource, it will seem mystical to the practical-minded—but then anything that cannot be moved by a bulldozer is likely to seem mystical to them." He urged that we consider "some other criteria than commercial" when it came to putting aside wilderness lands, stressing open spaces not just as a counterbalance to "our insane lives," but as something integral, and vital to, our national character.[35] I would argue that we have to nurture that same love for the wild world closer to home for similar reasons, reasons that have nothing to do with the practical and reasons that at times might be beyond, or below, words.

The simple fact is that being outside, being in so-called nature, is a joyous part of being human and, it would stand to reason, of being any sort of animal. Most of us do not like being caged. The natural world offers us delight and love, and freedom. Whether this converts us into do-gooders or not depends perhaps on temperament and genetics, and anyway is really beside the point. The very fact that being in nature causes this reaction is enough. More than enough; it's a reason to celebrate. I am not suggesting that we send our children out into the woods with protest signs. I'm suggesting we send them out so that they can learn about delight and spontaneity, and learn what a wildly diverse party is (still) going on out there. Hopefully a few of them—nine out of a hundred, say—will end up handing out leaflets. But if fifty others just get a little hint that there's a world beyond screens and walls then that is good enough.

Of course, as Stegner points out, to fall for something in the world—let's take a flower, for instance, the most obvious and cliché of nature icons—is also to invite scorn from the purely practical-minded. But follow these passions, without the approbation of others, and you may have what Thoreau called "unexpected results." Then again, you may not. You may head to the peak-oil hills or become a ranter or dogmatist. You may become lazy and abandon your family to lie around smoking pot in a field of lilies. These are possible outcomes, but, I would argue, not likely ones. It has been my experience that those who actually make nature part of their lives, as opposed to those who theorize or write policy about it, tend to have their minds stretched a little and their perspectives widened. They also tend to laugh a little more and to build muscles of nonconformity, developing the capacity to love it even more. And while that doesn't save the world, it isn't such a bad result.

The goals that I have set out may seem too modest given this time of crisis. I do not prescribe them for everyone. If you are a scientist on the verge of inventing an anti-global warming laser beam, please do not give it up to fight for your local flower bed. But for the rest of us there may be no global solutions. For the rest of us the best we can do it to tackle a project of self, something that excites our imagination and marshals our limited forces. Which is not to say that that project of self should be un-ambitious. Think of Thoreau's project of knowing Concord, which included its plants, creatures, and its seasons. Think of Dan on the river. In fact, you could argue that any project worth its salt should be beyond your reach, grand to the point of stretching you beyond yourself. I have talked to many scientists over the last couple of years and as it turns out, many of their projects now include ways in which the ecosystems they work with will adapt to the changes wrought by climate change. The point is that everyone's project is different. But all the best projects excite, incite, ignite, all that.

Even if you agree with this premise that we all need a great project of self, you might still ask: Why can't a self project that focuses on the stock market be just as vital, just as absorbing? Why does this answer have to include Nature?

Maybe because it always has. Maybe because, despite what Nordhaus and Shellenberger say, it is not thanks to post-affluence that we are interested in the "environment," but because it is our home and has always been our home. It is where we evolved and where, if we are very, very lucky, we will keep evolving. And to reintegrate it with our lives, even in the smallest of ways, can be a stroke of personal genius.

Which brings me, finally, back to language. One of the things that gets in the way of making nature, even limited nature, a part of our lives is the way we talk and think about it. While I have argued with Nordhaus and Shellenberger throughout this book, I agree that we need to shake out some of the old myths, to beat the rug with a broom and let the dust fly. Our new language needs to be more open, less school marmish and less fuddy-duddy. We need to throw out the bunk. We need nature lovers who are more hard-nosed and direct, but also more wild and more willing to tell new stories that stir people. What will drive post-material man? More money? A bigger house? I don't think so. I'd like to imagine that that man or woman, his or her basic needs met, might look for something deeper than that. I'm not just talking about a life of buying all green consumer products. Sure, a smaller car and a smaller house are a good start, but I'm talking about something more than green underarm deodorant or green toilet paper, something that can start with spending a part of your life getting outside into the world and getting to know your non-human neighbors. If that sounds modest so be it: For my part I've noticed that when I put my body outside my mind tends to follow. What I'm tossing out is the possibility that a life intertwined with the non-human, a life intertwined with the wild, provides both a more stirring story and a better life. Yes, I said "better." Not just wilder, not just more moral and more fun, but also, though we're not allowed to say it in this age of relativism, *better*.

Maybe one reason so many of us keep going back to *Walden* as if it were a sacred text is that we get to spend time in the presence of a young man, a cocksure and bold young man, who by doing things exactly his own way struck some sort of gold. The gold is still there for all of us. I first picked up Thoreau's book when I was sixteen and I don't think I've ever recovered. Henry ruined my life, but in a good way. I was hungry for something different, something authentic, and that is what I found.

Maybe that's who I've really been talking to in this book: the sixteen year old I was then and others like him. Maybe I want to ruin his life all over again. And I want to ruin your life too. I want to put forward the crazy notion that hoarding money, and that hitting computer keys that move that money from one pile to another is not the road to fulfillment during the brief time we're here. In its stead I want to suggest falling in love with the world, and maybe battling to alter it in some small way, while radically opposing the perception that humans are the only important thing in the universe. To suggest that we are just a part of a world of plants and trees and animals and mountains and seas and rivers. As it turns out fighting for these convictions is, by happy coincidence, both a fulfilling way to be and an obvious good. So here's my final word to that sixteen year old who used to be me.

Go get 'em.

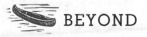 BEYOND

I sleep on Dan Driscoll's couch and commute in to work
with him the next morning. Since getting a lift on his
handlebars is impractical, he decides to drive today and
we head down a littered and war-torn Storrow Drive.
We park near the dam to the harbor and Dan chats with
the parking guy for a while. This is another side to Dan,
one I didn't see on the river, the man-of-the-people side,
and it continues when we cross a small park and run
into a state maintenance worker. He is a big guy, easily 6'4", and the two men greet each other like long
lost relatives. A little while later, after I say goodbye to
Dan, I double back and talk to the man. I ask him about
the perception of Dan within the state government.

"He's not like a lot of government people," the guy
admits. "I guess sometimes he rubs people the wrong
way. Even me sometimes. Sometimes I want to say, 'Dan,
stop bugging me.' But he's persistent. That's the only
way to get things done. And Dan gets things done."

The sun is out and I have a whole day in front of me.
Later I'm meeting my wife and daughter to explore the
Charles in an entirely different way: by duck boat. Duck
boats are a big tourist draw, amphibious vehicles that
travel through the streets of downtown Boston before
plunging into the river. The highlight of the trip will be
when the gruff captain lets Hadley, all of four, take the

wheel. For now though I content myself with an older means of travel, walking the couple miles along the river from downtown to Cambridge. A massive morning effort is underway to take down the stages and pick up trash from the previous evening. Four hundred thousand people were gathered here last night but now I have good stretches of the river to myself. I follow the wending water, the robin-egg blue dome of Harvard's Eliot House acting as my snooty beacon. After about a mile I come upon a spot where I used to take my lunch when I worked as a carpenter in downtown Boston. I wasn't very fond of my life at the time, and sought out the water as refuge.

For the most part I stick to the river, with only one detour. I hike inland and over to Fenway Park. There's a night game but the bustle of preparation is already in full swing, and when I see a tour group heading in one of the Lansdowne Street gates, I file in behind them. Then, at gate C, I slip away from the tour and sneak up to the seats. There's another urban nature book to be written about this place: the wilds of Fenway. Is there a better Boston moment than first seeing the grass and orange dirt, the jewel inside the city? (Not long after my trip, in fact, a pair of red tail hawks will take up residence in a nest below the press box, only to be unceremoniously evicted before opening day.)

Workers are hosing down the seats and a player is out running laps. In left field, the old wooden scoreboard reveals the season's narrative to date: We are eleven and a half games ahead of Toronto, and more importantly, twelve games ahead of New York. I make my way through the stands to the Green Monster seats. They are still relatively new and I've never sat here before, and when I get there I can't believe how steep and scary they are. I imagine reaching for a hotdog or beer and tumbling to my death in left field.

It takes only ten minutes to get from the Green Monster back to the river, or would if I didn't take a second detour. I climb down out of stands into the catacombs and exit discreetly through the bleachers gate, before heading to the Boston Alehouse for a beer and a lobster roll. From there I hike through the mess of Kenmore square, cut down Deerfield street, take a left on Bay, and head out over the footbridge. Back at the river it's a steamy day, haze rising off the Basin. My arms are sore from three days of paddling but I feel good. I take a seat on a park bench and look out at the water. I think it's fair to say that my relationship with the Charles has changed, maybe even deepened, over the last week. I watch the river flow out to the sea.

I close my eyes and picture Dan floating down from Waltham to Watertown. He navigates our leaky canoe through a wilderness partly of his own making. Maybe, I suggest to Dan from the front of the canoe, maybe fighting for a limited wilderness is the most vital fight of all, since most of us won't ever go to Everest or the Amazon. Maybe the most important wilderness is the one closest to home.

"Maybe," Dan half-agrees. "But maybe it doesn't have to be so limited. I see this as just a start. What if we connect this green corridor to the Mystic River and connect that to the Neponset? What if we have all these wild paths connecting all through Boston?"

What if?

I take in the world that Dan once envisioned, enjoying the light pulsating on the under branches of the maples. Meanwhile Dan's mind races elsewhere, no doubt imagining

weaving greenways all through the Boston area and beyond. As we drift toward the city, he plans and schemes
and dreams.

This is my manifesto. My attempt to nudge people toward
something, or back toward something. Toward what? An
understanding that most of us already have on a deeper
level. That a world exists outside of us. A world that
reminds us that we are animals, too, animals who have
evolved along with other animals on this earth. Thinking,
planning, scheming, talking, writing animals, but animals
nonetheless. This is an idea that, when we acknowledge
it, may at first make us feel smaller, but that ultimately
feels right, feels like it fits, because it has the advantage
of being honest. And while it may initially be depressing to admit that we live in a world where we decom-
pose in the ground, just like other animals, ultimately
it is freeing: a world full of possibilities, of wildness, of
hope. A world that I, personally, find it a joy to inhabit.

Of course it's a world worth fighting for, we've gone
over that. But it's also more. Because in the end we all
have concerns that are deeper than politics, even deeper
than the urgency of saving the world. These concerns are
also deeper than words. It is hard for a writer to admit
that words can't escort us to where we finally need to go,
that they can only walk beside us for part of the trip. But
words point beyond words toward the mystery of being
alive in this confused place, a mystery that each of us
tries to solve in a different way. Part of the mystery we
are trying to answer is "how to be in this world." I accept
that there are a thousand answers to this question, to this

essential query. But what I don't accept is any answer to that greater question that doesn't include nature. Because it has always been part of the answer, and it always will be. Because my love for nature is not the result of my post-materialist affluence but something encoded in me. And because you can put me in a spacesuit in a condo on Mars and I'll still dream of a rocky bluff back on Cape Cod.

POSTLUDE:
THE END OF THE WORLD

It's the end of the world, they say, but my response is the usual one. I'm paddling out to the island again. It is a little past dawn, almost exactly three years after my river trip with Dan Driscoll. Solstice was a couple of days ago and July Fourth is a few days off. Over the past month, I've been kayaking out here, to this empty barrier island, at least a couple times a week, leaving from the dock near our new rental house along the Carolina coast. If I hit the tide right, low enough so the motor boats can't get into the creek but high enough so I don't have to pull the kayak through the thigh-deep muck, à la the African Queen, then I have a world to myself. Myself and the birds. Specifically, egrets and pelicans and ospreys and oystercatchers and skimmers and herons of all stripes and, my new favorite, the ibises. The ibises spend their days literally poking around, that is poking crazy curved orange-red bills into crab holes in the marsh muck.

One of the best parts of this trip is slipping into the sinuous tidal creek that winds into the marsh, getting down low enough below the marsh grasses and oyster beds, and moving quietly — which is easy in a kayak — so the birds barely pay any attention, going about their business as I go about mine. Another of the best parts is landing here on Masonboro Island, which is populated only by birds, beach grass, elder bushes, sea oats, ghost crabs, a few trees

that weren't taken out by hurricane Hazel, and lately by a
fox family that has a den to the north on the wider part of
the island. After I pull the kayak up on the backside marsh,
I get to walk over the small hump of island's middle toward the ocean's roar. Which is really the best part of the
best part, hearing that roar and then, a few seconds later,
seeing the heaving waves of the Atlantic. Today, through
dint of my relatively minor effort of paddling, I have the
whole eight mile island to myself, which seems close to
miraculous in these crowded times. This morning the
water has taken on a green-blue Caribbean look, which
makes me laugh out loud, and I think, looking down at the
crescent of beach curving off miles to the north, that it is
like having my very own desert island. When I am feeling dramatic, which is often enough, this seems fitting: It
is here that I have found myself thrown up on the beach,
Crusoe-like, forced to start a new life in a strange new place.
I'm almost ready to plant a flag and claim it as my own.

I didn't expect to land here, in North Carolina, but I
have tried to make the best of it. We all need to find our
Waldens, wherever we are. Our own forts in the woods even
if we are (somewhat) grown up. When I look back on my
green manifesto, I see it as a kind of young adult or children's
book. It is naïve and goofy and overly romantic, but isn't
that where we need to start from if we have any shot of
connecting to the world? There's plenty of time later for
buttoning down and improving your portfolios. I now see
the trip down the Charles, and the thinking that went with
it, not so much as a pivot point in my life but the beginning
of a deepening of commitment. The last I heard, Dan had
fulfilled his dream of connecting the greenways on the
Charles to those of the Mystic and Niponset Rivers. The

world may be going to hell — and I am told tarballs may be
hitting these beaches soon — but I believe in my small patch
of wild, however limited. It is vital for me to get out here,
even if my place is not a pristine place or an ideal place.

Or even a solitary one. Today as the waves crash in
and slide back, and as the sun rises higher in the sky, I
notice something quite strange on the slope of half-wet
intertidal sand. Small footprints. A little child — six or
seven — has been walking here. There's no one around
for miles — I can look up and down the beach and see it's
empty — but there they are. The prints would have been
erased at high tide, which was about five hours ago at two
in the morning. So . . . was there a child out here roaming the island in the middle of the night? I have no idea.
What I do know, or assume, is that they are the footprints
of a little girl. "Do you have daughters?" asked a belea-
guered and crazed King Lear, assuming that his situation
was reflected in the world's. If I ran into Lear right now
I would answer his question with an emphatic yes. I have
a daughter, though I am pretty sure that these prints are
not hers and that she is home asleep at the moment.

But she has walked this island plenty. Often Hadley has
paddled out here with me, sitting in the front of the kayak,
better company even than Dan Driscoll. As soon as we land
on this beach, she is off and running, collecting shells and
chunks of conglomerate and running wild on an island
she thinks of as her own. Back home she has made maps
of Mucky-Gucky land, Oysterville, and Egret Island, all
names of her own creation. And we have seen some sights
here, sights I hope she will remember. One day we saw
an osprey with a fish in its talons sitting atop an oyster
bed like an ancient conqueror on a hill of skulls. Another,

we saw what I am almost certain was the same bird flying with an eel in its talons, a great silver strand hanging
down three feet or so. We have watched dozens of egrets
out on the mud flats, like a field of white flowers, and they
barely budged when we paddled up to them. And we have
learned about the strange ibises, how they eat fiddler crabs
in the salt marshes all year long, except after their young are
born when they fly inland to gather non-brackish crayfish
to feed their nestlings who are not yet able to digest salt.

As wonderful as those times were, I don't make any
claims for the permanence of the pastoral. In fact, if my
geologist friends are right, this island itself will be under
water by the time Hadley is my age. During moon tides it's
just a sliver of sand, and so at best it's a temporary Walden.
But I will take it while I've got it. The island is doomed, they
say, and so is the world. Screw that. This morning, out just
beyond the mysterious footprints, black skimmers mow
the surf and I am thinking about my little girl, experiencing
this world anew, and I am full of love. And hope, too. Don't
forget hope. Of course there is every reason to be hope-
less but what fun is that? I embrace the still-wild world.

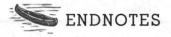 ENDNOTES

1. Ed Cobb, "Dirty Water," in *Dirty Water* (Los Angeles: Capital Records, 1966).

2. Charles D. Elliot, "Somerville History," in *Somerville Past and Present: An Illustrated Historical Souvenir*, eds. Edward A. Samuels and Henry H. Kimball (Boston: Samuels and Kimball, 1897), 25.

3. "A Backyard Wilds" is dedicated to Amy, as promised.

4. William Manchester, *The Last Lion: Visions of Glory 1874–1932* (Boston: Little, Brown & Company, 1983), 6.

5. Ibid.

6. Jack Turner, *The Abstract Wild* (Tucson: University of Arizona Press, 1996), 25.

7. Samuel Johnson, *The Works of Samuel Johnson, L.L.D.*, vol. 3 (Philadelphia, 1825), 165.

8. Ralph Waldo Emerson, *Essays and Lectures* (New York: Penguin Putnam Inc., 1983), 515.

9. In those days, McKibben seemed to me a powerful and slightly remote figure, tall and thin and archetypal, someone who, as another classmate recently put it, always looked a little like Abe Lincoln. The one time we actually interacted in college was when he supported me during the controversy that followed the publication of my cartoon, *The Trickle Down Theory*, which was a picture of Ronald Reagan urinating on an unemployed black man in the gutter.

10. Wallace Stegner, "Variations on a theme by Crèvecoeur," in *New West Reader: Essays on an Ever-Evolving*

Frontier, ed. Philip Connors (New York: Nation Books, 2005), 105–124.

11. Wendell Berry, *The Long-Legged House* (New York: Harcourt, Brace & World, Inc., 1969), 150.

12. Duane Hamilton Hurd, *History of Norfolk County, Massachusetts* (Philadelphia: J.W. Lewis & Co., 1884), 42.

13. Henry David Thoreau, *The Essays of Henry D. Thoreau*, ed. Lewis Hyde (New York: North Point Press, 2002), xii.

14. Ted Nordhaus and Michael Shellenberger, interview by Amanda Little, "An interview with the authors of the controversial essay, 'The Death of Environmentalism,'" Grist, January 13, 2005. http://grist.org/article/little-doe/

15. William Broyles Jr., *Castaway*, DVD, directed by Robert Zemeckis (Universal City, CA: DreamWorks, 2000).

16. James C. O'Connell, "How Metropolitan Parks Shaped Greater Boston, 1893–1945," in *Remaking Boston: An Environmental History of the City and its Surroundings*, eds. Anthony N. Penna and Conrad Edick Wright (Pittsburgh: University of Pittsburgh Press, 2009), 168–197.

17. To confuse things more, the MDC has recently morphed into the DCR, or "Department of Conservation and Recreation."

18. Richard Higgins, "Gradually, MDC gets back land along Charles," *Boston Globe*, August 10, 1997.

19. Joel Myerson, *The Cambridge Companion to Henry David Thoreau* (New York: Cambridge University Press, 1995), 96.

20. Jack Turner, *Abstract Wild*, (Tucson: University of Arizona Press, 1996), 99.

21. Ralph Waldo Emerson, *The American Scholar: Self Reliance and Compensation* (New York: American Book Company, 1893), 40.

22. Henry David Thoreau, *Walden and Other Writings* (New York: Elibron Classics, 2006), 624.

23. Robert D. Richardson, *Henry Thoreau: a Life of the Mind* (London: University of California Press, 1986), 376.

24. Henry David Thoreau, *Walden: an Annotated Edition*, ed. Walter Harding (New York: Houghton Mifflin Company, 1995), 94.

25. Charles Darwin, *The Origin of Species*, ed. Charles W. Eliot (New York: P.F. Collier & Son Company, 1909): 88.

26. Henry David Thoreau, *Walden: a Fully Annotated Edition*, ed. Jeffrey S. Cramer (New Haven: Yale University, 2004), 17.

27. Stephen Jay Gould, *Ever Since Darwin: Reflections in Natural History* (New York: W.W. Norton & Company Inc., 1977), 25.

28. Charles Darwin, *The Origin of Species*, ed. Charles W. Eliot (New York: P.F. Collier & Son Company, 1909), 527.

29. Henry David Thoreau, *Walden: a Fully Annotated Edition*, ed. Jeffrey S. Cramer (New Haven: Yale University, 2004), 12.

30. Stephen Jay Gould, *Ever Since Darwin: Reflections in Natural History* (New York: W.W. Norton & Company Inc., 1992), 257.

31. Michel de Montaigne, *The Complete Essays of Montaigne,* tr. Donald M. Frame (Palo Alto: Stanford University Press, 1958), 856.

32. Wendell Berry, *The Long-Legged House* (New York: Harcourt, Brace & World, Inc., 1969), 150.

33. Henry David Thoreau, *Walden* (New York: Harper & Brothers Publishers, 1950), 440.

34. Charles Darwin, *The Origin of Species*, ed. Charles W. Eliot (New York: P.F. Collier & Son Company, 1909): 529.

35. Wallace Stegner, "Wilderness Letter" in *Wilderness Reader*, ed. Frank Bergon (Reno: University of Nevada Press, 1980), 315–333.

David Gessner is the author of several books of literary nonfiction. His writing has been recognized with numerous awards, including the John Burroughs Award for Best Natural History Essay, and has been selected as Best American Nonrequired Reading. He teaches creative writing at the University of North Carolina at Wilmington, where he founded the award-winning journal, *Ecotone*.

More Nonfiction from Milkweed Editions

To order books or for more information, contact Milkweed at (800) 520-6455 or visit our Web site (www.milkweed.org).

The Nature of College:
How a New Understanding of Campus
Life Can Change the World
By James J. Farrell

The Future of Nature
Writing on a Human Ecology from Orion Magazine
Edited and introduced by Barry Lopez

Hope, Human and Wild:
True Stories of Living Lightly on the Earth
By Bill McKibben

Toward the Livable City
Edited by Emilie Buchwald

The Colors of Nature
Edited by Alison H. Deming and Lauret E. Savoy

Milkweed Editions

Founded as a nonprofit organization in 1980, Milkweed
Editions is an independent publisher. Our mission is
to identify, nurture and publish transformative literature, and build an engaged community around it.

Join Us

In addition to revenue generated by the sales of books
we publish, Milkweed Editions depends on the generos-
ity of institutions and individuals like you. In an increasingly consolidated and bottom-line-driven publishing
world, your support allows us to select and publish books
on the basis of their literary quality and transformative potential. Please visit our Web site (www.milkweed.
org) or contact us at (800) 520-6455 to learn more.

Donors

Milkweed Editions, a nonprofit publisher, gratefully
acknowledges sustaining support from Amazon.com;
Emilie and Henry Buchwald; the Bush Foundation; the
Patrick and Aimee Butler Foundation; Timothy and Tara
Clark; the Dougherty Family Foundation; Friesens; the
General Mills Foundation; John and Joanne Gordon;
Ellen Grace; William and Jeanne Grandy; the Jerome
Foundation; the Lerner Foundation; Sanders and Tasha
Marvin; the McKnight Foundation; Mid-Continent
Engineering; the Minnesota State Arts Board, through
an appropriation by the Minnesota State Legislature
and a grant from the National Endowment for the Arts;
Kelly Morrison and John Willoughby; the National
Endowment for the Arts; the Navarre Corporation; Ann
and Doug Ness; Jörg and Angie Pierach; the Carl and
Eloise Pohlad Family Foundation; the RBC Foundation
USA; the Target Foundation; the Travelers Foundation;
Moira and John Turner; and Edward and Jenny Wahl.

amazon.com   jer•me   Bush Foundation
              foundation

THE McKNIGHT FOUNDATION

MINNESOTA
STATE ARTS BOARD

NATIONAL
ENDOWMENT
FOR THE ARTS
A great nation
deserves great art.

TARGET®

Interior design by Wendy Holdman
Typeset in Dante
by BookMobile Design and Publishing Services
Printed on acid-free 100% post consumer waste paper
by Friesens Corporation

ENVIRONMENTAL BENEFITS STATEMENT

Milkweed Editions saved the following resources by printing the pages of this book on chlorine free paper made with 100% post-consumer waste.

TREES	WATER	SOLID WASTE	GREENHOUSE GASES
36	16,705	1,014	3,468
FULLY GROWN	GALLONS	POUNDS	POUNDS

Calculations based on research by Environmental Defense and the Paper Task Force.
Manufactured at Friesens Corporation